Erik Ringmar is Professor at the National Chiao Tung University, Hsinchu, Taiwan. He is the author of *Interest, Identity & Action* (CUP, 2007) and *Surviving Capitalism: How We Learned to Live with the Market and Remained Almost Human* (Anthem, 2005), as well as many academic articles in the fields of history, international politics and sociology. He received a PhD in political science from Yale University in 1993 and between 1995 and 2007 he taught in the Government Department at the London School of Economics and Political Science. He lives deep in the Taiwanese mountains surrounded by gorgeous females (one wife, four daughters). He is a Linux user, a Bob Dylan fan, and likes to eat roast duck. His next book, *The Fury of the Europeans*, deals with imperialism in China in the nineteenth century.

Erik wrote his first blog entries in January 2006. Two months later his university, the LSE in London, insisted he 'take down and destroy' his blog.

A Blogger's Manifesto

Free Speech and Censorship in the Age of the Internet

ERIK RINGMAR

ANTHEM PRESS
LONDON · NEW YORK · DELHI

Anthem Press
An imprint of Wimbledon Publishing Company
www.anthempress.com

This edition first published in UK and USA 2007
by ANTHEM PRESS
75-76 Blackfriars Road, London SE1 8HA, UK
or PO Box 9779, London SW19 7ZG, UK
and
244 Madison Ave. #116, New York, NY 10016, USA

British Library Cataloguing in Publication Data
A catalogue record for this book is available from the British Library.

Library of Congress Cataloguing in Publication Data
A catalogue record for this book has been requested.

ISBN-10: 1 84331 288 3 (Pbk)
ISBN-13: 978 1 84331 288 8 (Pbk)

1 3 5 7 9 10 8 6 4 2

Printed in the EU

Contents

Acknowledgements

My sincerest thanks to Ines Amezaga, Rodney Barker, Felix Berenskoetter, Aubrey Blumsohn, Michael Buehler, Douglas Bulloch, James Caspell, John Chalcraft, Sun Chipen, Lin Chun, David Cole, John Dale, Eman Ebed, François Gemenne, Leda Glyptis, Martin von Haller Groenbaek, Gur Hirschberg, Jonathan Hopkin, Bob Hunter, Nazir Hussain, Su Jingbin, Charles Jones, Sid Kamath, Sun-Ju Lee, Toby Lloyd, Oliva Lopez, Fatima Manji, Robin Mansell, Sara Martini, Wang Meihong, Qalandar Memon, Song Nianshen, Brendan O'Leary, Francisco Panizza, Benjamin Partridge, Diane Pranzo, Cecily Raynor, Gareth Rees, Yaz Santissi, Rana Sarkar, Jeff Weintraub and Liang Yoyo.

This book is dedicated to all my students at the LSE and especially to James Caspell, David Cole, Nazir Hussain, Sun-Ju Lee, Fatima Manji, Song Nianshen and Su Jingbin. Western civilization is safe in your hands.

'Don't ask me nothin' about nothin'
I just might tell you the truth.'
Bob Dylan, 'Outlaw Blues', 1965

1

'Watch It Buddy, I'm Blogging This'

'Hello world! This is Erik speaking. Is anybody out there?' It was 9 January 2006, and I was writing the first post in my very first blog. I had downloaded the software a few minutes earlier and now I was already up and running. *Forget the Footnotes* seemed like an appropriate name for it. Academics always add footnotes to give authority to their ramblings, but in my blog I was going to ramble without such props. 'Testing, 1, 2, 3, 4.' Well, I thought, the sky is not falling in, the computer is emitting no smoke. I'll just write and see what happens. I cleared my throat, dried my fingertips on my trousers, and started typing.

A funny thing happened at work today. One of the more pompous of my colleagues – Oxbridge education, plummy accent, egg on waistcoat – was giving a particularly tedious talk. Suddenly he drew something on the blackboard. An impromptu map, I think, but at this stage I was no longer listening. He continued speaking but turned around repeatedly and added to the map. For each addition the picture began to look more and more like a penis. After a while there was no doubt. There it was: a perfectly formed manhood in all its fully erect glory. Testicles, pubic hair and everything. I began laughing. First a little snicker, then a louder guffaw. Heads turned in my direction. I reported my observation to the person next to me who made a disgusted face. How dared I! Not funny. Not funny at all.

It was childish of course. Very childish. Both to laugh about it at the time and to blog about it later. 'I can't write that', I thought, 'my colleague is too easily recognizable.' Then again the joke was mainly on me, not on him. If I chose to be childish in public, it was my decision. Besides, this is a free country, right? I can say what I like. And I did.

Emboldened, I unleashed my childish wit on my boss, the big cheese himself, the Director of the university where I worked. I made up a story about Sir Howard Davies, a few choir boys and the Catholic Church. None of it was true of course – it obviously wasn't true – but just to be on the safe side I added an official, but faked, denial. It was, however, pretty funny. Brits are famous for their sense of humour. Sir Howard Davies is a Brit, ain't he? He can live with it.

After these posts I was exhausted. I didn't know there was so much childishness in me and now it was all over my blog, in public and for everyone to see. For better or worse, I had spoken. From the laptop on top of my bed in my home in north London I had spoken to hundreds of millions of people scattered throughout the world. Except that I hadn't really. My blog at this point was getting a mere dozen visitors per day – my family mainly and the occasional student.

Unfazed by the low visitor number, I felt that I had acquired new powers. The power to hurt and upset people and the power to make a fool of myself. But also the power to tell truths, to expose and reveal what I saw around me. The pretentiousness of colleagues, the corruption of bosses, the vile habits of family and friends. I'm going to turn myself into a blogging machine, I thought, reporting everything I see straight into cyberspace. The mighty will tremble, the powerless will take heart. 'Watch it buddy, I'm blogging this!'

Of course I knew there were limits to what I could say. There are always limits to what one can say. Legal limits, limits set by embarrassment, by fear or by an old-fashioned sense of decency. How exactly these limits should be defined, however, I did not know. Normally when you present something in public, there are editors who answer such questions for you, but in my blog I was my own editor. I had no experience, no policy, no guidelines. I, together with millions of other bloggers who simultaneously had taken up the habit, was flying by the seat of my pants.

Helicopters overhead

These questions became urgent a few weeks later when a Danish newspaper, *Jyllandsposten*, published cartoons of the Prophet Muhammad in various, shall we say, less than flattering contexts. The Danes, not unreasonably, insisted on their right to publish whatever they damn well pleased. But some Muslims declared themselves offended and took the opportunity to rant about the perfidy of the infidel West. The Danish embassy was set ablaze in Damascus, large demonstrations were held in Lebanon, and Danish products were boycotted throughout the Middle East.

The question was whose side the rest of us were on. Were we in favour of freedom of expression or did we believe in the obligation not to offend? It was a classic case of liberalism versus multiculturalism, the European Enlightenment versus political correctness.

Some newspapers in Germany and France reprinted the cartoons as a gesture of support for their beleaguered Danish colleagues.

British newspapers didn't, obviously so as not to complicate relations with the country's sizeable Muslim population. Still some Muslims in the UK were most irate. Demonstrations were held outside the Danish embassy in London on 3 February 2006, where young men, dressed as suicide bombers, issued direct threats. 'Behead the one who insults the Prophet', 'Europe you will pay, your 9/11 is on the way.'

As a newbie blogger I decided to be more courageous than the British papers. I was going to stand up for the Danes. A quick Google search and a 'save picture as…' – command and I had the offensive cartoons on my site. I had no desire to offend the Muslims, and I'm all for common decency, but death threats against those who publish cartoons was a step too far. If death threats are issued against us, our rights are taken away. If our rights are taken away, we must fight for them. This was not the time for decency. Suddenly, I had the *obligation* to publish those offensive cartoons. Someone had to stand up for freedom of expression. It might as well be me.

Well, these were the arguments I used when talking it over with my wife. As a non-blogger with her feet more securely planted on the ground, she pleaded with me. 'Why, oh, why? Our neighbourhood is predominantly Muslim. People around here are nice and friendly with each other.' 'What if our neighbours find out? What's the point of offending these good people?'

One night trucks loaded with explosives were racing through my head. Scimitar-wielding madmen were beheading my children. I woke up in a cold sweat. Somewhere high above our house there was a helicopter. Its persistent chop, chop, chop told me that the police was looking for someone. Of course, those irate young men who demonstrated outside the Danish embassy! I had read about the police chase and now they were in my neighbourhood. What better place to hide for a scimitar-wielding madman than in my Muslim part of the town?

I took the cartoons off the blog. Of course my wife was right. It wasn't worth it. I never liked the pictures anyway. They spoke in an aggressive visual language which wasn't mine. It was a defeat to be sure, but it was a defeat of no significance. The only casualty was my image of myself as a defender of Western civilization. Someone else had to stand up for the freedom of expression. Someone with a bigger blog and more courage. I was too scared.

In the first couple of weeks of its existence my blog had taken me for quite a ride. I had made fun of a colleague and my boss, exposed myself to ridicule and to the possible ire of some people in my neighbourhood. I had been transformed from being an quixotic defender of Western civilization to a self-confessed fool in the space of a few days. My blog was starting to seriously affect me. Was it really worth it? Why, after all, blog? Before I had properly answered these questions, things suddenly got a lot worse.

The republican promise

In the back of my mind throughout these first weeks of blogging was a half-remembered promise. Something about freedom of speech and the value of publicity. In Britain, in Europe, and wherever democracy has taken hold, people have the right to express themselves freely. This is a core freedom, I had been told, a fundamental right, a cornerstone of modern society. As a blogger, I enjoyed the full backing of modern civilization. World history and natural reason were on my side. Surely good enough.

After having read more, I came across three separate versions of this promise: a republican, a liberal and a radical. Although the three emphasized upon slightly different arguments, they lent each other strong support.

The idea of freedom of speech is an invention of the Enlightenment of the eighteenth century. At the time educated members of the upper-classes met in *salons* and coffee shops to discuss politics, the arts and the latest gossip. These groups were referred to as 'polite' or 'civil' society, and it was they who first identified freedom of speech as a matter of human rights. Not surprisingly, they spent most of their time talking. Their conversations constituted a 'public sphere', a shared space located outside the purview of individuals but also outside the purview of the state.

Although the members of polite society were upper-class, the conversational ethos which governed the public sphere was thoroughly egalitarian. The rules of conversation meant that everyone should have a chance to talk and that everyone would have to listen. *Égalité* and *fraternité* guaranteed the *liberté* of expression. 'I detest what you write', as Voltaire put it, 'but I would give my life to make it possible for you to continue to write.'

As the members of polite society explained, free and frank conversations have a number of beneficial consequences. Through conversations people become acquainted with unfamiliar views and experiences; they discover flaws in their own arguments and strengths in the arguments of others; they learn to take others into account, to moderate their views, and to become more realistic and practical about their application. The eventual conclusion of a public debate is always going to be far more intelligent than anything individuals can come up with on their own. Reason is a collective and not an individual achievement.

After the French Revolution, politics was recreated in the image of this conversational culture. Polite society transformed itself into a republic where all men were brothers and all enjoyed equal rights, not least the right to speak and publish freely. As the French 'Declaration of the Rights of Man and of the Citizen', adopted in August 1789, made clear:

> The free communication of thoughts and opinions is one of the most precious rights of human beings; all citizens can thus speak, write and print freely, except when abusing this liberty in cases determined by the law.

Similarly in December 1791, the first generation of Americans – another band of republican revolutionaries – revised their constitution to make sure that freedom of speech was adequately protected. The First Amendment reads:

> Congress shall make no law respecting an establishment of religion, or prohibiting the free exercise thereof; or abridging the freedom of speech, or of the press; or the right of the people peaceably to assemble, and to petition the Government for a redress of grievances.

The well-being of the republic, French and American revolutionaries insisted, depends on people's ability to talk, argue and exchange ideas. This is why freedom of speech is necessary.

The liberal promise

Nineteenth-century liberals affirmed these promises and added their own. For them the well-being of the community mattered less than the rights of each individual. Or rather, the well-being of the community could only be assured if individuals' rights were properly protected. And individuals, they believed, can only flourish if they have an opportunity to express themselves freely. Everyone should have a chance to pit their arguments against the arguments of others. This is how you develop your personality, become a particular someone rather than just another voiceless member of a faceless crowd.

The classical statement of this view can be found in John Stuart Mill's *On Liberty*, 1859. Today, Mill's defence of the freedom of expression reads like an early and rather quaint draft of a bloggers' manifesto:

> The peculiar evil of silencing the expression of an opinion is, that it is robbing the human race; posterity as well as the

existing generation; those who dissent from the opinion, still more than those who hold it. If the opinion is right, they are deprived of the opportunity of exchanging error for truth; if wrong, they lose, what is almost as great a benefit, the clearer perception and livelier impression of truth, produced by its collision with error.

Societies make progress, Mill believed, as errors and misconceptions are exposed, and as alternatives are proposed which can take their place. The more freely people can express themselves, the more secure we can be of our convictions, and the more rapidly society will make progress.

Of course some people may speak offensively or irresponsibly, but the best protection against such excesses is more free speech. It is not good enough for someone to claim that he or she is offended. Too many people are offended by too much. In particular, members of the elite are very easily offended when they can't come up with a good argument to justify their privileges. To ban offensive speech, Mill believed, is to protect the status quo.

The liberal view, combined with the republican, is paraphrased in Article 19 of the United Nations' Declaration of Human Rights, adopted in 1948:

Everyone has the right to opinions without interference and to seek, receive and impart information and ideas through any media and regardless of frontiers.

Or in the European Convention on Human Rights, adopted in 1950:

Everyone has the right to freedom of expression. This right shall include freedom to hold opinions and to receive and impart information and ideas without interference by public authority and regardless of frontiers.

The radical promise

But more radical promises were also made. What really matters, radicals argued, is not people's right to express themselves as much as their right of access to information. People in power will always cloak themselves with secrets in order to protect their privileges. Yet, freedom of speech has the power to reveal such shady shenanigans. Freedom of speech should above all be understood as a right to reveal what the powerful want to keep secret.

Compare the idea of 'enlightenment' as it was first introduced in the eighteenth century. To 'enlighten' is to throw light into darkness, it is to expose the secret and to clarify the obscure. Reason can't operate behind locked doors or in smoked-filled rooms; reason is always public, never private. Arguments which cannot be disclosed are for this reason necessarily suspect. Secrecy protects incompetence, prejudice and corruption. In the full light of publicity only such inequalities will remain which can be rationally defended.

Compare the etymological connection between the 'secret' and the 'sacred'. The sacred was always set apart. The face of God was always hidden and for that reason all the more terrifying. Priests were speaking in a mysterious lingo, performing rites which were awe-inspiring precisely because they were so terribly arcane. The Divine was inaccessible, indeed inaccessibility is what defined and constituted the Divine.

For a very long time politics had been thought of in much the same manner. In the Renaissance statecraft was considered a black art, an *arcanum imperium*, into which only the select could be initiated. And in the twentieth century, secrecy was more than anything what defined the totalitarian regimes. You never knew when the secret police would knock at your door; you were never told why you were arrested or where they were taking you.

Freedom of speech inoculates us both against religious prejudice and political repression. Freedom of speech serves transparency and disenchantment. Governments must be accountable, and if God can't stand the light of day, he's in serious trouble.

Woodrow Wilson, the US President, was a radical in this tradition. Wars, Wilson believed, are more than anything the result of the secret machinations of statesmen. In a democracy young men can't be asked to die for reasons which aren't made public. Similarly peace, if it is to last, must be concluded through public negotiations:

> Open covenants of peace must be arrived at, after which there will surely be no private international action or rulings of any kind, but diplomacy shall proceed always frankly and in the public view.

Promises broken

This is what we were promised. The republican revolutionaries promised us a society where everybody can participate as an equal in political debates, and where everyone has a voice and an audience. The liberals promised personal growth, the right of all citizens to develop their arguments, skills and individuality. The radicals promised freedom of speech as a way to expose prejudice and corruption.

These are great ideals. Wonderful promises. Too bad they weren't kept.

As it turned out ordinary people were never actually meant to take part in public discussions. For one thing, before the establishment of state-funded schools in the middle of the nineteenth century, large portions of the population simply didn't know how to read and write. Many of them could not even speak the language of the countries of which they ostensibly were citizens. At the time of the French Revolution, for example, only 12 per cent of Frenchmen actually spoke French.

Besides, a majority of the people lived very far away from the big cities, they read no newspapers, had no electricity, and in general they were too busy eking out a living to worry about the violation of abstract rights. And poor people weren't going to be listened to anyway. As Adam Smith pointed out in *Theory of Moral Sentiment*, 1759, you need 'leather shoes and a starched white shirt' in order to be taken seriously at a political meeting. That is, you have to be a person of considerable substance and means.

Looking at them again, closer this time, we see the republican revolutionaries as a bunch of aristocratic snobs who were united above all by their disdain for anyone who did not know how to behave in their *salons*. And the nineteenth-century liberals, John Stuart Mill included, were all thoroughly upper middle-class. When they talked about freedom of expression and self-realization they had educated people with property in mind, no one else. And as for Woodrow Wilson and other radicals of his ilk, they usually reneged on their promises of openness as soon as the opportunity presented itself.

'Of course', the elites would say, with a bit of a laugh, 'what did you expect?' It is all a matter of economic power in the end. In order to reach out to large audiences you need access to a newspaper, a radio or a TV station. 'If you really want to speak freely you'd better own one of these.' 'We call it a democracy but freedom of speech is regulated by the principles of the market.' And the media market, like other markets, soon came to be dominated by a very small number of very large companies.

The rest of us were left to plead with the editors. Every media outlet had an editor and the editors were the ones who decided what was 'newsworthy', 'fit to print', and how the real estate of the public sphere – column inches and airtime – should be allocated. Editors set the tone of public debates. 'No profanities please, no personal attacks or ungrammaticality.' It was all very proper, very bourgeois. The kind of freedom we ended up with eventually was the freedom that survived these editorial filters.

It was quite obvious what and who were excluded. People without education were excluded, and people with ordinary views, moderately well thought-through and somewhat incoherently formulated. The kind of people, that is, who make up the majority of citizens of any democracy. People at large were talked to, but they were never allowed to speak for themselves. Their views were represented by 'spokespersons' who mimicked what they took to be on ordinary people's minds. They were told what to think, how to vote, what to desire and what to consume.

There is a direct parallel here to the mechanism of representative democracy. Democracy was initially thought to be impossible in modern societies of vast size and complexity. It was impossible after all to get all people together in one place to vote. The idea of representation solved this problem. In a representative democracy we don't vote ourselves but instead for a representative who votes on our behalf. As a result, the political spectrum was radically reduced and many of the craziest, and most innovative, proposals filtered out. People became passive spectators of, rather than active participants in, the political life of their communities.

Elites have always wondered why ordinary people are so cynical about politics. The answer is of course that nothing but cynicism is left to people who always are treated as consumers, but never as producers or ideas and political platforms.

The internet revolution

The internet is changing all this. The internet revolution is giving voices to the previously voiceless and empowering the previously powerless. For the first time ever there are no editorial filters in place. No one intervenes between the speakers and their audiences. Real estate in the public sphere is no longer a scarce commodity and its price has dropped to close to zero. Anybody with an internet connection can for next to no cost become his or her own newspaper, radio or TV station proprietor. We can all speak freely and to a larger audience than ever before.

Today, for the first time ever, the promises we once were made have a reasonable chance of being fulfilled. Today there could actually be freedom of speech. The internet, just as the public sphere once described by the revolutionary republicans, is a remarkably egalitarian kind of place. The web page of the large multinational company, for example, is not necessarily more professional-looking than a blog run by the penniless critic of the same multinational company. On the web, just as in the ideal republic, it doesn't matter who you are, but only what you say.

The liberal promise of self-expression is just as easily fulfilled. After all, there are few better outlets for creative urges than a blog. First, we design and write the web pages, gather comments from the visitors and collect ideas from other blogs, then we add photos, podcasts and video clips. Meanwhile, we keep a keen eye on the visitor numbers, hoping for ever-greater audiences. It's fun, educational, and a great way to express ourselves. The blog is ourselves in cyberspace.

And consider blogging as a tool of enlightenment. Today, huge 10,000 megawatt floodlights are being turned on the corrupt, the prejudiced and the incompetent. In every organization there is someone with information to impart or a compromising anecdote to tell. Earlier these stories only got past the editorial filters if they concerned important political issues. Now even the smallest injustices are easily publicized. If you don't like the new car you bought, tell the world about it. If you don't like your new boss, let colleagues, and prospective colleagues, know. If you are afraid of being found out, blog anonymously.

In this way, the secrets which sustained the injustices of the past are one by one being revealed. Beans are spilled all over the internet, whistles are blown, fingers are pointed. Hypocrites are forced to confront their hypocrisy; fools their foolishness. For the first time there is a real possibility that politicians can be held accountable, that private businesses can become transparent, and that religion will be stripped of its mumbo jumbo.

In the age of the internet, Eve could never have convinced Adam to eat from the tree of knowledge. 'I don't care much for apples', he would have said, 'besides I've got a new broadband connection'. And Doctor Faustus, rather than selling his soul to the devil in return for a few pathetic truths, would have posted the questions on his blog. Before long God himself will have to take up blogging if he wants to answer his critics. Everything which can be revealed will soon be revealed. Woe to those whose lives cannot stand public scrutiny.

Return of the thought police

The reactions of the old elites reveal their hypocrisy. The people who used to control the editorial filters can't accept that their monopoly now is gone. They saw themselves as official custodians of the public sphere, yet their position rested on nothing more than the existence of a particular kind of technology – printing presses, radio and TV. Now that there is new technology, the nature of the public sphere is changing, and their position of power is being undermined. Of course the old elites don't like it. Of course they really, really hate it.

'Freedom of speech is crucial', they say, 'but not for you, not for ordinary people, for people who speak plainly, irreverently or irresponsibly'. 'We were always prepared to die for people's right to disagree with us in public, but you are disagreeing in the wrong way. I'm not dying for you.'

The problem is that ordinary people use the internet as they themselves see fit. Chat-rooms are treated as locker rooms, blogs speak the language of confessions and 'don't-tell-anyone' confidences. People, in short, are treating the public sphere as though it were private. They are incoherent, repetitive and ungrammatical; they have no respect, no sense of decency, no commitment to reason or truth.

The old elites are giving their game away. The only people they really respected were other members of the old elite, people who had automatic access to the public sphere – mainly other proprietors of media outlets and those lucky few who got past the editorial filters. But who is now prepared to defend the right of secretaries to blog about their bosses, students to blog about their teachers, social cases to blog about their social workers, prisoners to blog about those with keys to their doors? Or the right of any other under-the-boot underlings to blog about those who lord over them?

In theory perhaps. Members of the old elite still give plenty of after-dinner speeches extolling the virtues of free speech. But you just wait until they themselves become the target of a blogger's new-found powers. They'll foam at the mouth and start calling out for censorship.

What we never realized before is that there is one kind of speech for the powerful and another kind for the rest of us. Instead of free speech we have constrained speech, speech hiding behind the cloak of anonymity, speech carried on in the fear of retaliation, speech which results in reprimands and sackings, speech which lands you on the blacklists of bureaucracies, corporations and schools. Yes that's right, bloggers are today being threatened, intimidated, silenced and fired from their jobs. It's legal and it's becoming increasingly common.

We expected this kind of treatment from repressive regimes. But repressive regimes are the easy cases. These regimes make no secret of their secretiveness and their repression. Democracies are supposed to be different, but in practice it is not always clear where the differences lie. Modern liberal society has revealed a face which very few of us previously have seen.

Should we be cowered? Should we back down? Hell no! Let's instead call them on their bluff. Let's remind the republicans, the liberals and the radicals of the promises they once made to us. Let's insist that our societies live up to the principles they profess to embrace. Working men of all countries, blog! And working women too, and unemployed bastards, and everyone else who has a grudge, a bean to spill and a story to tell. You have nothing to lose but your gags.

Free speech in the age of the internet

Yet, the question still remains what you can and cannot say in a blog. Forget the clumsy interventions of the thought police, forget the minute-to-midnight attempts by the old elites to protect their privileges. Their credibility is shot and we must be suspicious of their laws and regulations. If they tell you to stop blogging, or to blog differently, don't listen.

Still the question remains and somehow or another we'll have to answer it. What indeed can you say in a blog? What if you use it to get back at a girlfriend who left you, or a boss who turned you down for promotion? What if you pass on false information about a political opponent or a rival corporation? What if you spread unverified rumours and outright lies? What if you blog about the lack of preparedness of your military unit or the bargaining position of your company?

In the past we never had to answer such questions. Very few people had access to the public sphere and everywhere there were editors who answered the questions for us. Or rather, when we asked ourselves such questions in the past they always referred to the private rather than to the public sphere. It was a matter of what we could tell our friends, colleagues and family members.

Now the private sphere has invaded the public sphere, and has radically changed it. More equal access is surely a great thing, but this is not to say that we necessarily approve of all its consequences. Do we really want to live in a society where everything constantly is being revealed? What about our sense of privacy and, to use an old-fashioned word, our sense of propriety? We know how these questions were answered in the era of regulated, filtered, speech, but how should they be answered in an era of truly free speech? This book is my investigation of this issue.

code wasn't actually very difficult, but it took time and was often aggravating. You had to upload the pages to a server and the formatting was distinctly WYSINWYW (what-you-see-is-never-what-you-wanted). Most people couldn't be bothered.

This changed in 1999 with the creation of the first online blogging sites, websites which host pages that users themselves can set up. They are free and very easy to use. Here no internet literacy is required, only regular literacy, perhaps not even that. On sites like *Blogger, Livejournal, Xanga* and *Blogspot* you can be blogging in a matter of seconds. You compose text much as you would in a word processor but your words don't go into a file but instead straight out into cyberspace. With some luck, one writing session results in one post, and as individual entries are added to each other an ever-longer trail of posts is created.

For more advanced users there is free, open-source, software like *WordPress* and *MovableType* which must be installed on a web server. You upload the software and configure it to fit your needs. The advantage is that you become your own webmaster. You can add and subtract features to your blog as you see fit, changing layouts and adding plug-ins. No one can mess with you.

Other descriptions could go into the definition of a blog but they are less essential. Blogs are, for example, usually written by individuals, although team-written blogs exist too. Yet blogs are emphatically not just another official web page. First since they have trails of entries posted on different dates, but also since they are written by identifiable authors and often in a very casual tone. The language of blogs is conversational and often it's irreverent and kick-ass.

Blogs are often interactive, meaning that readers can contribute their own input to them. Most commonly this is done through the comments which readers leave after a blog entry. But some blogs also have chat-forums, bulletin boards or so called 'shout boxes' attached to them. On popular blogs these interactive features are often the most active, and most interesting, sections.

What is and is not a blog is sometimes unclear. Social networking sites – meet-and-greet sites like *Facebook* or *MySpace* – or educational software like Moodle, often have built-in blogging features, and discussion forums can have threads which effectively operate as a person's individual blog. A CMS or 'content management system' is a software package which organizes the material put on a web page. Some CMSes are effectively blogs and some blogs are effective CMSes. The blog format is constantly evolving, adding new features, and shedding the staid and solitary format of the first online journals. Even *YouTube* – the video site – is easily transformed into a vlog, or video blog. Just upload your clips and you're done.

The blogosphere has unclear borders, and while that may be annoying to those who keep a count of the number of blogs, it's one of the features that makes blogging exciting. Indeed, the term itself may be on its way out. Blogs are already a bit 'so eighteen months ago'. But that's not the point. The point is that we now can publish whatever we like online without interference from the editors who used to police the public sphere. The internet has given us all virtually costless access to a worldwide audience. The blogging format will change, but the self-publishing revolution will continue.

How many bloggers are there?

As the internet revolution took off in the first years of the new millennium, the number of bloggers grew exponentially. Since 2002 the number of blogs has doubled every six months. In April 2007, about 120,000 new blogs were created every day, or on average 1.4 blogs per second. *Technorati*, one of the archivists of the blogosphere, tracked some 70 million individual blogs worldwide. If there are one billion internet users, this means that one in fifteen is a blogger.

Interviews with bloggers describe the same revolution. The Pew Internet & American Life Survey found that in 2002 only 3 per cent of adult American internet users had a blog. Two years later the figure was 5 per cent, and in 2006 some 8 per cent, or 12 million Americans, kept a blog. In addition, a fifth of American teenagers said they had created a blog.

These numbers need to be adjusted both up and down. For example, the statistics tend to focus on blogs written in English and other widely spoken languages. People who blog in Laotian, Xhosa or Tagalog may not be counted.

The numbers should be adjusted downwards first since not all blogs necessarily are created by humans. There are robot-made blogs, for example, created for the single purpose of generating spam and links to other websites. *Technorati* claims to exclude spam blogs in their count, but it is unclear how successful they are since spam blogs may be difficult to distinguish from the real thing. Much of the blogosphere is a Bladerunner universe made up by machine-generated content.

In addition, the number of blogs doesn't correspond to the number of bloggers since some bloggers maintain several blogs. 10 per cent of American bloggers say they have more than one blog. Furthermore, not all blogs are actually all that active. It is not quite clear how to count a blog which is updated only occasionally, or at what point a blog should be declared dead.

Although the stats for the US are impressive, the most active bloggers in the world are the French. In 2006, some 60 per cent of French internet users visited a blog every month and 12 per cent said they had created their own. There are more bloggers in China than anywhere else – the estimate is that some 16 million Chinese have their own blog.

Who is blogging?

Everyone is. Well not really, but all kinds of people are. As a subset of all internet users, bloggers are better educated than the population at large, they are also more likely to live in suburbia, to be students or have jobs with computers on their desks. In several respects bloggers are the avant guard of the internet. They have used it longer than regular internet users and they use it more heavily. Bloggers are people who spend much of their day, and their lives, online. In some cases the blogs function as their virtual homes.

And as we have seen, blogging is a worldwide phenomenon. In April 2007, the largest number of blog posts, 37 per cent, were written in Japanese, closely followed by English at 36 per cent and Chinese at eight per cent. All other languages combined made up the remaining 19 per cent.

Bloggers are as likely to be men as women, although some studies report a majority of females. Interestingly in the US, white male bloggers are *under*-represented as compared with general internet users. In fact they are seriously under-represented. Only 60 per cent of bloggers are white, compared to 74 per cent of the internet users. While African-Americans are slightly over-represented, Hispanic-Americans are heavily over-represented.

Yet, the most striking difference is that generally bloggers are younger than other internet users and far younger than the population at large. More than half of them are under 30. Conversely, only one in ten is over 50 years old.

But this probably isn't very surprising. Blogs are often cutting-edge and in-your-face, they are informal and don't take themselves too seriously. Of course white, middle-aged men are likely to stay away. In fact, less than 10 percent of the bloggers are white, middle-aged males. If you want to fix an image of the average blogger in your mind, think 'teenage girl', not 'pompous git'. Or think of a 'person without other means of publicly expressing him or herself'.

How often do bloggers write?

If all blogs worldwide were updated every day, there would be 70 million daily blog posts. The actual number, however, is 1.5 million which indicates that not all bloggers are all that active. In fact, the number of daily bloggers must be even lower since some hyper-active bloggers post many – in some cases very many – times a day.

According to the Pew Internet Survey, typical American bloggers spend five hours per week tending their blogs. Some 13 per cent say the blog is 'very important' to them and a 'big part' of their lives. The same proportion also update their blog on a daily basis. Next to half of all bloggers post only once every few weeks or even less often.

It is fun to set up a blog and to write the first entries, but it might not be as much fun to go on writing on a daily basis. Often the blogger's muse cannot be summoned and as a result the page is updated less and less frequently. The shores of the internet are littered with blogs which have run aground and been abandoned by their owners.

How many readers do blogs have?

Again most of the hard information comes from the United States. According to Technorati data from April 2007, no fewer than 22 of the 100 most widely read web pages are blogs. And the Pew Internet Survey indicates that in 2006 some 39 per cent of the internet users read blogs, corresponding to no fewer than 57 million adult Americans. This represents a vast increase over the two previous years. As late as in 2004, a majority of those surveyed said they did not 'have a clear understanding of what a blog is'.

For an individual blog it's possible to gather all kinds of interesting statistical information. For example:

- how many people that visit the site – per day, per hour, per minute or second.
- which pages they read and for how long.
- who links to the site.
- what site that took them to the blog.

- the search-engine search terms that led them to the site.
- the IP addresses of the computers that visit the blog.

Keeping an eye on the stats, you'll learn a surprising amount about your readers. You may, for example, realize that your boss always logs on to read your stuff during his lunch break, that you have a large following in Malaysia, and that people, inexplicably, land on your site after entering 'Santa Claus rough fuck' in Google's search window.

Many bloggers don't know the statistics of the traffic on their sites, and those who do generally don't have many visitors at all. A majority of blogs are read by less than ten people per day, mainly by close friends and family. Only around 10 per cent have more than 100 hits per day.

The reason for the low visitor numbers is usually the same as the reason for the low sales figures for poetry or academic publications – most of it just isn't very interesting. Too many blog entries contain arcane references, maddening jargon and inside jokes. Most of what's written is only relevant to family members and friends or members of the same profession. Many blogs are websites only a mother could love. OK, let's be honest about it – most blogs are *shite*.

But what's important is often not the number of readers but rather who the readers are. If you keep a blog which collects information about the history of your family, say, it is surely good enough if your family members read it. For a blog about a certain school, you don't need to aim for more than the school's students. In some cases, one reader might be enough to make it all worthwhile. Imagine a blog where you write about your long-lost father – and imagine him one day discovering it and leaving comments under your entries. The visitor numbers are low but also high enough.

But not all bloggers are labouring in obscurity. There is a blogging elite, perhaps some 4,000 blogs, which together capture the vast majority of all readers. The most successful of these – the

'A-list' of bloggers – can get several hundreds of thousands of visits per month. Thanks to advertising and sponsored links they may even be able to live off their art. The world's most popular blog, by the way, visited some 68 million times, is maintained by the Chinese actress Xu Jinglei.

Beyond this glamorous blogging elite, the readership tapers off very rapidly indeed. The head of the blogging movement is very small, if curiously inflated, and the tail is endlessly long.

How does a blog find a reader?

An obvious problem is how readers and writers can meet up. From an author's point of view a blog entry resembles a message put into a bottle and tossed into the sea. Delivery is uncertain and most bottles end up at the bottom of the ocean. You never know who's going to read your stuff.

From a reader's point of view, however, finding a blog is rather the needle-in-haystack problem of discovering something worthwhile among all the dross. The obvious solution is a search-engine like Google or Yahoo which include blogs among all other web pages they catalogue. In addition, Google has a web page dedicated exclusively to blogs and there are engines like *Technorati* and *Icerocket* that specialize in blog searches.

Search-engines, however, are a pretty crude tool. Before a reader finds a blog he or she must plug in the right search terms and scroll through pages upon pages of suggested sites. A much smarter solution is to rely on links that refer a reader back to your site. If the links are put in conspicuous places, or in contexts where they make sense, the curiosity of readers will quite automatically be aroused. A click later and they'll be on your site.

Another way is to join a network which unite bloggers who share some certain concern. *BlogHer* is a website that lists female bloggers; *Iraq Blog Count* lists Iraqi bloggers; and *Scienceblogs* unite blogging scientists. In all cases, the sites are linked to each other and if you like one blog it's easy to find more blogs like it.

But you can also plant links yourself. You can, for example, go to *The Guardian*'s website and leave your internet address as a comment under one of their blog-based articles. You can even try to smuggle a link into *Wikipedia*, the online encyclopedia that anyone – including any blogger – can help edit. The most effective way, however, is to convince one of the A-list bloggers to link to you. If you're lucky enough to get such an endorsement, you can just lay back and watch the audience figures soar.

Since they are crucial for determining the size of the readership, links have a monetary value. Popular blogs can charge for the links they create and some people are prepared to go to quite some lengths to make people link to them. Compare the expression 'link whore'.

What do bloggers write about?

When mainstream media discusses blogs they usually refer to the ones that provide comments on political or social issues. These are the serious, grown-up, blogs in which professional pontificators strut their stuff. But such blogs are not the most common. Most blogs are not concerned with politics or activism but instead with whatever everyday events take place in their authors' lives. Blogs are journals, they aren't journalism.

The topics covered are very diverse. To make the term more manageable, blogs are sometimes divided into different subcategories. There is no fixed nomenclature here but these are some of the more common labels:

- *Advocacyblog* – a blog founded in order to spread a certain political or social message.
- *Anonyblog*, or *anonoblog* – a blog run by an anonymous author.

- *Audioblog* – a blog that predominantly includes audio files and podcasts.
- *Bizblog* – another name for a 'flog'.
- *Blawg* – a blog maintained by a legal professional focusing on the law.
- *Celeblog*, or *celebrityblog* – a blog focusing on one or several celebrities.
- *Doppelblog* – a blog which copy the content off other blogs while claiming it as original material.
- *Edublog* – a blog with educational content.
- *Eventblog* – set up in connection with a particular event.
- *Filterblog* – blog that gathers links to news stories and commentaries from other blogs and from mainstream news media, while adding its own reflections. Filter blogs often have a political content.
- *Flog* – from British slang meaning 'to sell'. A blog maintained by a company in order to sell a product or service, often under the ruse of being a blog maintained by an individual.
- *Kittyblog* – blog preoccupied with mundane content, such as one's cat.
- *Milblog* – a blog written by a soldier, such as the blogs written by soldiers in Iraq and Afghanistan.
- *Splog* – a blog set up for the sole purpose of gaining links, search-engine ranking, or promoting a product or website, that adds no value to web content as a whole.
- *Spoofblog* – a blog pretending to be the blog of a particular person, usually a celebrity or politician.
- *Vlog*, or *vog*, a 'videolog'. A blog maintained in the form of video clips, often physically hosted on external websites like *YouTube*.

In addition, there are a number of blog genres named after their authors: *pundit blog* – blog maintained by wannabe op-ed writer; *professor blog* – blog maintained by a professor; *WoaCE blog* – blog maintained by a 'woman of a certain age'; *pompous git blog* – blog maintained by pompous git, etc.

Is there freedom of speech in a blog?

Of course not. In a blog, the blog owner reigns supreme and this reign may be just as draconian as ever the rule of the editors of traditional media. Blog owners can easily delete posts with which they disagree; they can change comments posted by someone else or post their own comments in someone else's name. You can even generate a vigorous debate on your blog all by yourself by assuming different identities.

Some blogs have carefully written-up statements regarding their editorial policy where they describe how they deal with comments and what kinds of things you can and cannot say. Other blogs have no official policy and contributors to the site can find themselves arbitrarily censored. Tough luck.

There may be good reasons for such practices. All blogs get spam for online sex, Viagra or Swiss watches. The point is usually to make blog readers click on links to these sites and thereby help boost their page rankings. Excluding such comment spam is both legitimate and necessary.

In addition, there are trolls. Trolls are readers who leave inflammatory, off-topic, or otherwise inappropriate comments on a blog so as to get a reaction from the ordinary readers. Who should be designated a troll is completely up to the blog owner. Creationists are trolls on Darwinian websites and vice versa. Once you've been identified as a troll you may be subject to various humiliating treatments designed to drive you away. Your comments may be deleted, arbitrarily rewritten or have their vowels extracted from them. 'Fucking bastard' becomes 'Fckng bstrd'. Some blog owners decide that the best policy against trolls is to ignore them. Hence, the acronym 'PDFTT' seen on some sites – 'Please Don't Feed the Trolls'.

Freedom of speech is thus unlikely to exist within an individual blog but happens instead between blogs. If you're banned from someone's website, you can always set up your own. On the internet trolls too have full freedom of expression. In fact, much of the blogosphere resembles a virtual Scandinavian forest where trolls and other shady creatures are wreaking terrible revenge on their enemies, real as well as imaginary.

How anonymous is a blogger?

A majority of bloggers decide to write anonymously or under a *nom de blog*. Some like the mystique of a secret identity, others prefer to create an on-blog persona which is distinct from the off-blog person they consider themselves to be. Anonymity gives you more freedom to make up stories and to tell tall tales.

Most importantly anonymity gives you the freedom to speak freely. A *nom de blog* protects you from repercussions, it means you can't be identified, censored, reprimanded or fired. Friends, family and colleagues may have their suspicions of course but if you don't reveal too many personal details you should be OK. As a result people say things in anonymous blogs they would never dare say in the offline world.

Anonymity makes blogs different from other public media. True, journalists have always protected the anonymity of their sources and newspapers sometimes have gossip columns written under pseudonyms, but in a blog it is possible to completely hide your identity or to completely misrepresent it. Straight, white, middle-aged men can turn themselves into young, lesbian, black women. They can even post the photos to prove their identity.

Differently put, anonymity means that you don't have to take responsibility for what you say. You can call people names and give free reign to your racism, sexism or antidisestablishmentarianism. Some of your readers are bound to be offended by such forthrightness while others will be excited to find that someone else shares their prejudices. Suddenly, words that no one would have dared utter have become parts of our public discourse. The very act of publication lends them a measure of legitimacy.

It is certainly possible for a government or a particularly sneaky employer to crack a *nom de blog*. If you pay for your blogging account or your email server, your credit card details will reveal where you live. The easy way around is to sign up for blogging accounts and email services that are free – preferably ones located outside your country. The IP address of the computer you're using when blogging can also be traced. This is a reason to always blog from public computers in libraries or internet cafés. In addition, there are a range of evermore sophisticated techniques for avoiding detection, from proxy servers to internet tunnelling and blogging by encrypted email.

The last of these techniques is only for the truly paranoid or for those who insist on the freedom to blog in countries like China or Iran. It is technically possible for bloggers to avoid being detected even by repressive governments such as these, although full anonymity will make blogging into a far more complicated business. In practice, however, there is always a risk of being detected.

How do you tell fact from fiction?

The biggest problem for an anonymous blogger is credibility. In the offline world we judge trustworthiness by assessing the people we come into contact with. The better we know a person, the more credibility they have. People we don't know ourselves, we judge through the credentials they can present. We trust doctors or lawyers since they are certified by their peers and by the government.

On the web it is next to impossible to judge people, and this is particularly difficult in the case of bloggers who remain anonymous. The whole point of anonymous blogging is to sever the connection between the online and the offline persona. As a result, we have no idea if the author really is who he or she claims to be.

For a bean-spilling or whistle-blowing blogger this presents a dilemma. Anonymous blogging assures one's freedom to speak but it also undermines the credibility of one's message. The damaging revelations don't sound all that different from the eccentric ravings of a mythomaniac. And the more damaging one's message, the less likely the readers are to believe it. Frantically demanding that people trust me, trust me, trust me, only make matters worse.

The way to deal with this problem is to reveal as much as possible about yourself. The more information your readers have the easier it is for them to judge you. If you take the step of disclosing your offline name, this information can be independently verified. It helps a great deal if you can attach some professional acronyms behind your name – a PhD, OBE, MoD or IOU – or an affiliation to a well-known company or educational institution. 'Trust me', the blogger says, 'I teach at Stanford University'.

Blatantly self-promotional blogs can never be anonymous. At least if the self you want to promote is the one in the offline world. This is why academics, authors, actors, singers, lawyers and computer experts usually blog under their own names.

The importance of offline credentials means that many of the power hierarchies created in the offline world come to be imported into the blogosphere. It is not only the power of your argument that counts in the end but also who you are, where you work and perhaps even how much money you make. The blogosphere is not the community of equals which the republican revolutionaries of the eighteenth century promised us.

The problem for bean-spilling and whistle-blowing bloggers is of course that anything they say which increases their trustworthiness is going to make it easier to identify, and hence punish, them.

But it is also true that blogs can establish their own credibility. A regular reader of a blog gradually learns to judge its author, even if he or she remains pseudonymous. The informal tone of most blogs help in this regard. Evermore cynical about commercial and political messages, web-surfers are likely to trust bloggers simply because of their ungrammatical sentences and their general edginess.

In a world filled with slick communicators, we are likely to give more credibility to rough messages. 'Shit', says a blogger, 'it's Monday morning and my boss is going to humiliate me again.' Of course we believe him.

How do you stay out of trouble?

Anonymity is one way of staying out of trouble but there are other techniques. In fact 'how to blog safely' guides have developed into something of an independent literary genre. The basic advice here is not to say or do anything that is controversial, likely to offend anyone or reveal your true identity. When in doubt, say the guides, take the blog down or clear it with your boss first.

This is bad advice! This is advice derived from the old obsequious world of editorial filters where ordinary people shut up and left the talking to their representatives. What's the point of blogging if you can't say anything offensive? What's the point of a right to free speech if you can't use it?

It's much better to write whatever you feel like writing – controversial, offensive, in-your-face – and then do whatever you can to confuse the thought police and throw them off your scent. Blogging technology presents some interesting possibilities here, especially if you use your own software on your own server.

An obvious first thing to do if trouble strikes is to take the site down. This way you can claim that it never existed. When the boss has stopped cursing himself for not making an offline copy, you can put it back up again. Under a new name and at a new location. You can also change the material at a moment's notice. In contrast to a newspaper, where every word remains indelibly for all future, the words in the blog disappear when you delete them. If your boss complains, change the text around and claim it never was there in the first place.

The problem with both these techniques is that your web page may be stored – or 'cached' – in other places on the web.

Google maintains an enormous cache of old pages and there are websites that specialize in archiving old versions of the internet. Still, these back-up systems are far from comprehensive and chances are your boss doesn't know about them anyway. Take a bet on his ignorance and deny everything.

In a variation of this technique, you can change the text back and forth randomly or according to some predetermined pattern. Perhaps you discuss the blatant case of police corruption in your town only between 8 and 10 p.m. every evening? Perhaps, the truth about your sadistic co-worker only comes out during every lunch break?

Or you could have two blogs, one official, maintained in your name, the other unofficial and anonymous. In the unofficial blog you propagate all kinds of outrageous slander and in the official blog you quote from the unofficial. Naturally you make sure to deny any personal knowledge of the allegations, perhaps you even try to rebut them. Denying and rebutting, you still give publicity to the rumours and help spread them around.

Alternatively, you provide different access to different users. Casual web-surfers see one version of your page, registered users see another version, and a select group of insiders see something completely different. Or vary the message depending on the IP addresses of the computer used by your reader. In this way instead of a desperate cry for help coming from your dorm room, your mother, when she logs on, is greeted with a happy smile and a request for more chocolate chip cookies.

Blogs are a great way of 'coming out' of whatever sexual closets you feel yourself trapped in, but why come out to everyone at once? If you are a Muslim woman studying in Europe, you may, for example, want to block information about your sexual liberation for all users coming from a particular country in the Middle East. Or if you are a Catholic priest blogging about the need to use condoms to prevent the spread of AIDS in Africa, block access for computers coming to your site from the general Rome area.

Why blog?

The most interesting question is perhaps why people bother. Why, after all, blog? But considering how easy it is, and how much fun, you might as well turn the question around. 'You don't have a blog? Whaddayamean you don't have a blog?' In the online world, not having a blog is like not having a face in the world offline. 'If everyone is claiming their identity, why aren't you claiming yours?'

Naturally, people blog for all kinds of reasons. Perhaps they have a political, religious or social agenda which they want to promote or perhaps they are simply trying to stay in touch with family and friends. In surveys, a majority of bloggers identify very general reasons: 'I want to express myself creatively' or 'I want to document my personal experiences' or use the blog as 'a storage site and memory device'. That is, blogs are more than anything a means by which we describe and explain our lives to ourselves. Blogs are means by which we create and narrate our identities.

This explains why a majority of bloggers insist that they blog mainly for themselves. It is not that they don't realize that others may be reading, yet this attention is quite coincidental to their online projects. Compare the reason why people keep offline diaries. By writing down our thoughts we externalize them, make them into things which exist outside ourselves. As such we can relate to them as we relate to other objects in the world. Putting ourselves into writing we come to understand ourselves better.

Online blogs add exciting new features to this age-old preoccupation. All identity-creation requires an audience. We must be recognized by others before we can be someone. Or rather, we make up stories about ourselves which we test on the various audiences we address. The internet turbo-charges this logic of recognition and makes it into a fun-filled and action-packed video game. In our blog we are not limited by our offline endowments and our anonymity makes it is easy to play around with self-descriptions. Pretense comes naturally and so does make-believe.

Perhaps you feel unsure about your sexual identity. Come out in a blog and see what it's like before you come out in your offline life. If it's true that all humans are 20 per cent homosexual, use the internet to create a more complete identity for yourself – set up five blogs and give your gay side its due in one of them.

All writers always have some readers in mind. The particular thrill of online writing is that it's easy to see these imagined audiences as real. In your mind the ex-girlfriend hasn't actually forgotten you, she is still there, secretly reading your every word. And you aren't actually letting your boss walk all over you, you are standing up to him in your blog, and he too is a reader. You're not a powerless low-life living in a trailer park. Blair and Bush – or at least their advisers – are closely monitoring your assessment of the situation in Iraq.

This is why people are surprised when they get into trouble for blogging. They knew there was an audience out there but it was always *imagined* as real, not really real. This is also why disciplinary actions against bloggers always are experienced as great insults. The external world intervenes into your fantasy, disrupts it and informs you in no uncertain terms that some kinds of dreams are *Verboten* and some imagined identities out of bounds.

Some blogs – by pundits, professors and pompous gits – would seem to have little to do with such identity-creation, but of course that's not really the case. These blogs are superficially about current events, but their real topics are their authors. The blog is where you make yourself into an authoritative person, a source of information and insightful analysis. A long-haired, middle-aged, professor might use his blog in order to affirm his identity as an eccentric outsider still in touch with his student. This too is a kind of dreaming, a fantasy-creation which the blog helps make real.

3

Free Speech and Censorship at the LSE

After all the excitement of the first month of writing, I was looking forward to some peace and quiet. The entries about penis-drawing colleagues and scimitar-wielding Muslim madmen were archived by my blogging software and neatly stashed away behind a hyperlink where only the truly curious would find them. I began looking for new subjects. It was easy. Academics after all make a living out of pontificating. Give us today's headlines and we'll give you an instant lecture. It's like a pretentious version of 'Just a Minute' – except that academics deviate from the subject a lot, and endlessly repeat themselves.

Instead of news commentaries, however, I decided to use my blog for assorted critical asides. Lecturing and writing requires you to take on an official persona. You pretend to be a voice of authority, an expert, someone with unique and invaluable insights. Yet, this is of course only so much play-acting. Most of the time a majority of academics are about as ignorant and insecure as your average Joe (or Joanne). In a lecture or in a book you can never admit this, but in a blog you can. My blog became my private confessional; ad libbed comments muttered to the people seated in the first row. 'I should have prepared better for the lecture this morning.' 'I can't stand grading exams.' 'I never actually read *Being and Time*, you know, I only pretended to.'

Such admissions are surely perfectly innocent. Yet in the context of English academia, they turned out to be surprisingly subversive. Much like the monarchy or the church, English academia relies heavily on secrecy and mumbo jumbo in order to legitimize its position in society. Secrecy and mumbo jumbo protect the university from being inspected by outsiders and they instill a sense of awe in the general public. Critical asides and innocent admissions tend to ruin the mystique.

And maybe that's why I went on doing it. I was never big on academic pretentiousness and I never understood why some academics take themselves so extraordinarily seriously. I decided to use my blog to do something about it. To open a few doors and to kick a few butts. To turn my critical faculties on myself and the institution — the London School of Economics, LSE — where I worked.

Why is it, for example, that no one ever talks about how much money academics make? Surely, such secrecy only benefits the employer. Each employee can be made to think that they make more money compared with others when in reality they make far less. In this way, one person is pitted against another. As a modest contribution to the class struggle I published my salary – in pounds and pennies – online. Yes, students were amazed that an academic didn't make more. On the other hand – and I made this point as well – English academics don't really work more than about five months in a year. The remaining seven months are referred to as 'research' – that is to say, a bit of reading, a bit of interviewing, and a lot of buggering off. Yes, buggering off became the topic of another blog entry.

Next came student fees. The LSE is highly dependent – one could say addicted – to student fees. If the government can't feed us, the students have to. Student fees have gone up dramatically in the ten years since I started at the LSE, and there is no doubt that PhD students in particular are being overcharged. For the 12,000 pounds they fork out they get little more than a few chats with an absent-minded supervisor. Many PhD students can't afford to remain in London and end up going back to whatever country they come from. Sitting somewhere in Bangladesh, Botswana or Bolivia, desperately trying to finish their PhDs, they transfer what most likely is the equivalent of their family's combined yearly income to the LSE and to the British economy. Very generous, one could say. Like an aid programme in reverse. Or perhaps it's just really, really stupid. Well, that's what I said in the blog anyway. 'Kids, whatever you do in life, don't do a PhD! Or at least do one in the US where you get generous funding and proper PhD-level courses!'

Considering the price of an education, the very least one can expect is that the university provides prospective students with adequate information. If an education is to be sold like so many sausages, universities should be forced to declare what kind of meat, artificial colouring and pig fat the courses contain. An obvious step is to make the course evaluations of previous years' students available online. According to the university authorities, there are a thousand reasons why this cannot be done, but they all come down to a fear of the truth. Bad teachers will be named and shamed, and so will bad universities. Again, I decided not to wait for official permission. My blog had given me the opportunity to put my student evaluations where they belonged – at the fingertips of prospective students.

Another topic was the strange ethnic mix of the Government Department where I worked. Of the 49 full-time academic staff, including tutorial fellows and lecturers on temporary contracts, there were 16 professors out of whom 14 were English and only two non-English. Conversely, out of the non-professors, 25 were non-English and eight were English. In other words, the non-English get hired but for some reason the English keep the professorships for themselves. It seems that the English establishment, in my Department as elsewhere, rely on imported, exploited, foreign labour to do the dirty work for them. 'The professoriate constitutes a club', I concluded.

> As all clubs they are ruled not primarily by intellectual principles but instead by social psychological. Above all it is important to make sure that no one rocks the boat. This is difficult to assure since, famously, all professors always are at each other's throats. This is why it is important only to include people who are like the already existing club members. Picking people with an Oxbridge background assures that a semblance of peace and order is maintained. It is at Oxford and Cambridge after all that you learn the 101 of gently nodding while ferociously stabbing each other in the back.

My Open Day speech

Are you allowed to say such things about the place where you work? And are you allowed to say them in public? I clearly thought so at the time, and I still do. After all, what else could freedom of speech possibly mean? Obviously public criticism is not encouraged in most ordinary workplaces, but universities are different. No university, surely, could be critical of critical thought? Certainly not the LSE? Innocently, I put a link to my blog in the signature of all my emails. Some people clearly clicked on it since my blog by this time began picking up readers – a dozen or so a day.

But it was offline rather than on that the shit eventually hit the fan. Real fan, real shit. On 22 March 2006, I gave a speech at the 'Open Day' – a recruitment event – organized for prospective LSE students and their parents. No, I wasn't the best person for the job. Yes, I had been at the LSE for ten years, and I had taught various undergrad courses, but I never really bothered to learn anything about the undergraduate degree as such. Panicking a bit in the morning before the speech, I tried to wiggle out of the responsibility, but the Convener of my Department, Professor George Philip, told me to rely on the official information pack I had received. I was to be the 'face' of the Department, Philip said, and a 'reassuring academic presence'. All that was needed 'is someone who knows how to operate PowerPoint'.

This was bad news. What the event required was obviously someone with a sales pitch. Someone who could tell the official story of the School and the Department the way it should be told, and convince prospective students to choose the LSE over its rivals. This, after all, was the first year that undergrads were going to pay real money for their education. Per head they would bring 3,000 pounds to the ever underfunded institutions of higher education. In this situation we were asked to swallow our pride and take the money. 'Fire up PowerPoint and start flogging the wares.'

Problem is, I'm not very good with PowerPoint, I'm not a 'face' of anything except myself, and I never aim to provide 'reassuring presences'. Above all, I'm not a salesman. I don't approve of the commercialization of higher education and I resent the fact that academics are asked to deliver sales pitches. My views on these matters were all over my blog, but George Philip was clearly not one of my regular readers.

Since there was no way to get out of it, I decided to give the speech, but to do it my way, the only way I know how – to speak as truthfully as possible about what it's like to be an undergraduate student at an elite institution like the LSE. The point was not to slag off the School but to give prospective students a sense of what actual students have told me about their experience over the course of the years. The LSE is a great institution – I never questioned this fact – and surely, it should be able to use the truth as a recruiting tool.

Yes, I did mention that undergrad teaching comes very far down on the list of priorities of most LSE academics and that teaching alone will never give a lecturer a promotion. 'If you want a high-flying academic career you have to publish.'

This means that first-class teachers usually will have their minds elsewhere than on undergraduate teaching. They might be away on conferences, and even if they are not absent in body, they may be absent in mind.

To make things worse, I argued that the in-class experience of LSE students differs only little from the in-class experience of students at lesser universities. But as it turns out, I happen to believe that this is the case. And it's not difficult to explain:

The kinds of courses taught at undergraduate level are pretty much the same everywhere you go. The courses use the same kinds of reading lists, with the same kinds of books, set the same kinds of exam questions... The lecturers too are not that different from each other. More often than not we went to the same universities and it's only coincidence that lands us at the LSE rather than at, say, London Metropolitan.

What really makes the LSE different are instead the students. 'We are', I said, 'able to recruit some of the smartest, most interesting, intelligent, rich, successful and all-round attractive people on the planet'. This is the real reason why you should choose the LSE.

As an LSE student you will be a part of this extraordinary multicultural collection of bright and fun and ambitious people. These will be your friends and peers; you'll make girl and boyfriends among them. They are you! And for the rest of your life you will be a part of a network of LSE alumni spreading out across the globe.

The LSE's reaction

Returning home in the afternoon, I put the whole speech online and proceeded to blog about it. I didn't expect any reactions and I didn't get any. For a few days. Then there was an email from George Philip. As it turned out, an administrator from student recruitment – present at my speech – had denounced me to her boss, and her boss had been in touch with mine. An investigation was quickly put together and witnesses were called. What I had said, George Philip argued, 'departed from the prepared message'; I had 'embarrassed colleagues and discouraged prospective undergraduate students from applying'. He reprimanded me for the Open Day speech and for maintaining a blog.

The blog, he said, 'makes statements that are enormously damaging to your own reputation … and potentially damaging to the School'. For now, Philip hoped, an 'informal oral warning' would be enough, together with my agreement to first 'destroy/cancel your blog entirely and shut the whole thing down until further notice', and second 'when representing the School in the future, doing so in a positive way that does not risk bringing the School into disrepute'. Philip also asked me to apologize to a long list of people, including the staff at undergraduate recruitment.

At a loss what to do, I emailed the colleagues in my Department hoping for support. I was livid – at being censored by a member of the administrative staff, at being misrepresented, at being told to shut up. No one can tell me what to say in my own classroom – no secretaries, no convener, not the devil himself. Of course I didn't expect my colleagues to agree with everything I had written, but I did expect them to have a few Voltaire-style words to say about the right to freedom of expression. The big professors got back to me quickly and publicly and they all agreed with the Convener. Clearly, they concluded, I had overstepped the line and obviously there could be no such thing as a general right to blog. 'Enough of this juvenile posturing', these 'crass generalizations' and 'solipsistic ramblings in blogland'. I needed to 'get real'. If my comments were picked up by mainstream media they

> would be highly damaging to the Department's reputation for undergraduate teaching, and which if it were at all widely disseminated would be inimical to recruiting students and hence very clearly damaging for the economic life-chances of your colleagues in our joint enterprise.

> This is not about blogging, this is about willfully damaging the reputation of the Department and the good intentions of your colleagues.

> I completely disagree with your statement that faculty mainly care about their own research but I'm away on a conference right now and I don't have the time to comment in detail.

And even if the Department indeed did have some dirty laundry, why on earth was I washing it in public? 'I would suggest that you take down all the LSE-related aspects of your blog immediately while you ponder on the meaning of freedom.' 'In many institutions and many companies an employee who vilifies his employer and colleagues in the way you did would most probably be sacked. So consider yourself lucky.'

The consensus was not complete. There were a few dissenting voices. A couple of junior, and very courageous, faculty members defended my right to speak – although they carefully pointed out that they did not necessarily agree with what I had said. More support arrived in private emails. But the majority of my colleagues just kept their heads down. Why take a stand on such a controversial issue? Why risk antagonizing the very people who are in charge of promotions?

Hoping for a clarification of the rules that apply to bloggers, I contacted Sir Howard Davies, Director of the LSE. He didn't get back to me for a few days, but eventually there was an email. This is what he said:

> I entirely support your Convener's views. I looked at the blog and it seemed to me to be damaging to the School and to contain criticisms of your colleagues, and of the School's promotions procedures, which are inappropriate. You accuse the School of systematic discrimination against non-British staff which I reject, and you say teaching is ignored in promotion decisions, which I know to be untrue.
>
> Your further messages to your colleagues and to me are disingenuous. The issue here is not a policy on blogging, it is whether a colleague can publicly abuse his employer and his colleagues without consequences. I further understand that you repeated these slurs to parents and prospective students, which is further cause for complaint. I think you should reflect carefully on your behaviour which I find most disappointing.

I was shocked and suddenly very worried. But while my fears no doubt were justified, my surprise was not. Howard Davies has a background in business and not in academia. Before he came to the LSE, he was Chairman of the Financial Services Authority and Director General of the Confederation of British Industry. His instincts are those of a boss, not an academic. He gives orders and expects to be obeyed. Like many others in the English establishment he knows very much about rules and very little about principles.

Let's be clear about this. It is not that the LSE is opposed to freedom of speech as such. Not at all. In the fall of 2006, for example, one LSE academic made national headlines by predicting that human beings in the future will evolve into two distinct subspecies – the tall, genetic, elite and the dwarfish illiterates with low foreheads and even lower IQs. Meanwhile, another LSE academic argued that the problem of poverty in Africa is the result of the inferior intelligence of black people. In both cases, the LSE authorities were quick to stand up for the right of the respective academics to state their unpalatable views.

My mistake was to use the freedom of speech to discuss the institution itself – the LSE and English academia. Freedom of speech is fine, everyone including Sir Howard Davies agreed, but only as long as speaking freely did not deter prospective students from applying. In an era of commercialized education, the limits to freedom of speech are set by the market.

Neither George Philip nor Howard Davies ever retracted their threats and I remained under surveillance. There was an LSE computer that checked out my blog over 1,150 times, and there were several other computers that clocked up many hundreds of hits. These could of course have been fans of mine, but somehow I doubt it. This is not freedom of speech. You cannot think and write freely as long as you are afraid of intimidations.

It was all too much in the end. I'm not much of a fighter, I don't like confrontations with people in power, and I'm not used to taking on the English establishment. Reluctantly, and after much agony, I took the blog down.

Saved by my students

After a few days, however, defying my Department's ban and the threats made by the Director, I decided to put the blog back up. The reason was the reaction of my students. Students are always naive and often very idealistic. Give them a lost cause to fight for and they'll leap at the opportunity. They clearly believed all the hype about universities as centres of critical thought.

Very, very early one morning I sent my undergrad students a link to my blog. They, after all, are the only true authorities when it comes to questions of student experiences. I wanted to know if they recognized the description I had given. Only an hour or so later I heard back from the first student. She said she had just returned from a night on the town. 'WOAA MAN!' she screamed, 'finally someone who tells it the way it is. A teacher who has the guts to tell the truth about what all LSE students are thinking. Respect man, serious respect.' OK, I thought, she may be drunk, but I'm on to something here.

The first trickle of emails quickly grew to a torrent and the vast majority of messages echoed the initial one:

> I really enjoyed reading your Open Day speech. I think it was right on target. If the university has a problem with it, I can only imagine that it is because it is 'too' honest.

> I speak for nearly every LSE student I have met in endorsing wholeheartedly what was contained in your speech. ... Good luck, the students are with you all the way!

> Just read your speech, and honestly think it's one of the most accurate accounts of life in the Government Department that I've ever read. Most of it is also accepted truth among both students and staff in the Department, and to the extent that it's inaccurate, it's probably on the flattering side.

Several students also insisted that a realistic description of the university was more likely to recruit students than a slick presentation. 'We aren't stupid, you know?'

A small number of students were hostile. Some clearly felt that I had besmirched a university which they had made great sacrifices in order to attend. On the other hand, prospective students from as far afield as Nigeria and Mexico contacted me saying that my speech had encouraged them to choose the LSE.

One very entrepreneurial student created a petition on the *Facebook* website – 'In Support of Erik Ringmar' – and it soon had over 380 signatures. The LSE student newspaper, *The Beaver*, had an article about my case – 'massive student support for threatened lecturer' – and a very well-argued editorial which defended the right of academics to speak freely. Students of mine reported overhearing conversations all over campus with references to 'that lecturer in the Government Department'. And for a while I was, in the words of a teaching assistant with her tongue in her cheek, 'a student hero and an urban legend'. Now that's what I'll put on my gravestone!

That's where the *Guardian* and the *Times Higher Educational Supplement* picked up the story with headlines like 'A Blog Too Far at the LSE' and 'Lecturer's Blog Sparks Free Speech Row'. A spokeswoman for the LSE tried her best at damage limitation. My blog had contained 'offensive and potentially defamatory material', she explained, but magnanimously the School now 'regarded the matter as closed'. Yet most of the *Guardian* article consisted of long quotes from my blog. I came across as a lovable eccentric, my wife insisted, and in a public showdown between a lovable eccentric and a repressive bureaucrat, the lovable eccentric will always win.

At the bottom of my *Guardian* article there was a hyperlink to my website and before long the number of page hits soared. In a single day, on 4 May 2006, my blog had over 5,000 visitors. As an academic author you have many readers if you have 500, but now I had ten times that number in a single day. The really cool thing was that the hyperlink put me in direct contact with the *Guardian's* readers. I commented on the article in my blog and by clicking on the link they instantaneously got my reaction. The poor LSE bureaucrats were completely out of the loop. *The Guardian* couldn't link to them. They have no blog.

And then the blogosphere started buzzing. My website climbed the *Technorati* rankings and people linked to me from all over the world. The predominant reaction was surprise. 'Curious goings-on at the LSE…' 'A strange story just in from London…' '*Un exemple très drôle ici chez nos amis de la L.S.E.*' Chinese websites were interested in my arguments in favour of American grad schools and Malaysian sites wondered if English academia was losing its self-confidence. American websites just laughed and laughed and laughed. 'Trust a stuck-up tea drinker to fight for freedom? Where would y'all be but for the good ol' US of A?'

The hypocrisy of expertise

If I had worked at Wal-Mart or McDonald's these reactions of my employer would have made perfect sense. Wal-Mart and McDonald's are not in the business of promoting freedom of speech. The LSE, however, is. The School likes to present itself to the world as an authority in matters of civil liberties.

This noble tradition goes back to the LSE philosopher Karl Popper who in his book, *The Open Society and Its Enemies,* presented a powerful argument in favour of openness and critical thought. History, Popper argued, follows no predetermined course and society can only make progress as long as we are free to ask questions. At the time, during the Cold War, this argument constituted what perhaps was the most powerful weapon in the West's intellectual armoury.

Georg Soros, Popper's student at the LSE, redeployed these ideas when setting up his Open Society Foundation. Through his philanthropy, Soros supports independent newspapers, websites and civil society organizations throughout the post-Soviet world. Of course the LSE loves him, and Soros is a frequent visitor to the School. The LSE wants his money and I suppose he craves the intellectual legitimacy his alma mater can bestow.

The LSE is consequently full of civil rights experts. The School has a Center for Civil Society, a Center for the Study of Human Rights, a Center for the Study of Global Governance, in addition to the Law and Media Departments with their respective experts on new media and free speech. There are also authorities like the political philosophers in my own Department who make a living explaining the European tradition of liberal rights to undergrads from around the world. There is also a person like Andrew Puddephatt, who founded *Article 19,* an international human rights organization that promotes freedom of expression. You might even find Sir Howard Davies himself banging on about the importance of free expression. At least, if you catch him on a good day.

As one would expect, freedom of speech is well protected by LSE's statutes. The School's 'Code of Practice on Free Speech' explicitly incorporates Article 19 of the UN's Universal Declaration of Human Rights:

> this right shall include freedom to seek, receive and impart information and ideas of all kinds, regardless of frontiers, either orally, in writing or in print, in the form of art, or through any other media of his or her choice.

I'm not much of a lawyer but 'any other media of his or her choice' should surely include blogs. In fact, the LSE's code goes a couple of steps further and introduces a disciplinary procedure for those who prevent the free speech of others.

> Action by any member of the School or other person contrary to this Code, will be regarded as a serious disciplinary offense and, subject to the circumstances of the case, may be the subject of proceedings under the relevant disciplinary regulations.

It seemed pretty obvious to me that Howard Davies and George Philip were in violation of this code. In the summer of 2006, I lodged a formal complaint with the LSE's 'Free Speech Group'. One committee member got back to me saying he was away on vacation. After that there was no further communication from their end. I repeated my complaint right before Christmas 2006, this time with a copy to Howard Davies and to the student newspaper. I heard back from Howard Davies' secretary but never from the Free Speech Group itself. As far as Free Speech groups go the one at the LSE is very tight-lipped.

What is going on here? How can a leading institution of higher learning be so obviously hypocritical? I've pondered this question for a year now, and I think I finally have figured it out.

The problem is the LSE's status as a centre of expertise. Experts are people with in-depth knowledge of specific techniques or fields of scholarship. The solutions experts provide are derived from the theories they embrace. Such expert knowledge is what gives the LSE its unique position and its staff its unique pretentiousness. LSE's professors, they like us to believe, have answers to the questions asked by decision-makers the world over.

But it just doesn't work that way. Expert-driven social engineering has a disastrous historical record. Witness the problem of economic development or Third World aid. Often, the experts have little impact on the situation and occasionally they make the situation far worse. The reason is that theoretical knowledge just isn't enough. In addition you need local and hands-on knowledge, information about the situation on the ground. This knowledge is neither theoretical nor even possible to express in words. All local people know this and they make fun of the experts behind their backs. Once the experts fly home, they get busy rectifying their mistakes.

The LSE too – like all universities – contains a lot of local knowledge. You can't run the place according to abstract schema. You don't need theory but instead concrete knowledge of actual human beings and actual places and things. This is basically what everyone including Howard Davies was trying to tell me. This is what the oft-repeated admonitions to 'get real' came down to. Abstract principles are fine, they said, but don't overdo it. Someone, at the end of the day, has to sponsor our next research leaves.

This is why freedom of speech, as LSE experts see it, always concerns others. It concerns poor, faraway, or post-Communist countries. It doesn't concern us right here and now. This is also why freedom of speech is about big, important topics, but not about the mundane and trivial. Our expertise is something we apply to the outsiders; to ourselves we apply only local knowledge. We save the lofty principles for after-dinner speeches and rely on practical experience in order to get things done. This, I believe, is why most experts reveal themselves to be hypocrites, and why the LSE is unable to apply its own principles to itself.

Are they right about this? Must a university be run by rules rather than by principles? Are universities really different from other workplaces? We'll return to this question in the next chapter.

Learning my lessons

Instead of trying to close down my blog, my Department tried to dig up dirt on me. Clearly they were preparing some kind of a process. A well-placed source assured me that the Convener of my Department was convinced I had lost my mind, and rumours regarding my madness began circulating. For a while, I was banned from grading exams on account of my impaired judgement. A woman from Human Resources began asking detailed questions about an operation I had had a few years earlier. One day, a motorcycle courier delivered a confidential invitation to go on a disability leave. Needless to say, I declined. I was very angry, but I was not mad.

One of my teaching assistants reported:

> you might be interested to know that I recently received an email from [the Government Department] asking me the way to provide them with feedback about the way you were supervising undergraduate teaching (how often you met with me, whether you monitored me, etc.). I don't know if it is a regular procedure or a way of trying to intimidate you, but I made sure that nothing of what I replied could be held against you.

One day an email appeared in my inbox, circulated to everyone in my Department, detailing how I had let a certain undergraduate student down a year earlier and neglected my duties as a teacher and tutor. A disgruntled PhD student was also produced and he provided further evidence against me. There was going to be an investigation, a process, a disciplinary hearing.

It was standard bullying tactics, and pretty clumsily executed at that, but I didn't react at all well to it. In the end I was not courageously standing up for civil liberties at all, I was at home cowering under a blanket. The more they threatened me, the more defiant I became, and the more terrified. I stopped coming to work by mid-April, and by mid-May, I was no longer reading emails. By the end of it all I was too upset to even get back in touch with my friends and supporters. I held my office hours in Starbuck's and stole into my office very early in the morning to pick up mail. I didn't sleep enough, and I probably drank too much.

The situation was untenable of course. As a tenured member of the permanent faculty, it was next to impossible to get rid of me, but they had endless means of making my life unbearable. In the summer of 2006, I was fired from the LSE Summer School after working for them for some eight years. The Summer School had always provided a much-needed extra pay cheque, and the courses had been fun to teach. But this gig was not a part of my regular contract and once my blog became a national news story, I was not asked to teach there again.

In the fall of 2006, I went on a long-planned sabbatical and on 1 February 2007, I resigned from the LSE. I work at a university in Taiwan these days. Yes, I sort of fell off the map. Then again, Britain and the LSE don't show up very prominently on the mental maps of people here in East Asia. National Chiao Tung University, NCTU, in Hsinchu, is a world-class institution with a great faculty and ditto students. I brought my wife and my children with me of course and we are thoroughly enjoying ourselves, discovering the Taiwanese mountains, drinking papaya milkshakes, learning Chinese.

Best of all, my new employer couldn't care less what I write about in my blog. NCTU is not a commercial venture and they don't worry much about student recruitment. They take the curious view that university professors should have the right to say whatever they like, both in their classrooms and online. In general, Taiwanese democracy, introduced in the 1980s, is still young enough for people to take its values seriously. There are plenty of people around who remember risking their lives in defence of the right to speak freely. Yes, I'm still blogging, but no longer about the LSE or about English academia. There are many far more interesting topics to write about.

In the first year of its existence my blog had 97,467 visitors and some 12,543 people read my Open Day speech.

4
Bloggers @ Uni.Edu

Not all universities are as hypocritical as the LSE. Most have understood that the blogging revolution can't be stopped, and some have even understood that it is something that should be embraced. Universities are about communication, expression and criticism after all. That's what blogs are about too. The two go together like student dorms and disabled smoke alarms.

Still, most universities have been slow in grasping the magnitude of the transformation. Just take a look at the home page of any randomly chosen university. It's so obviously designed by consultants. You'll find a generic corporate site with pictures of engaged-looking professors in front of blackboards and groups of students – of suitable ethnic mix – smiling at each other on campus lawns. That's no way to communicate with the most web-savvy, and most cynical segment of the human population. People of blogging ages need interactivity, informality and plain truths. They need to know what the student experience really is like.

While clueless university administrators hire even more consultants to bring out even more generic-looking pages, the foot soldiers of the blogging revolution are reaching for their guns. Professors set up blogs on the sly and discover that they can use them for teaching as well as research, or simply for speaking their minds. Students are blogging too, but in addition, they are heavy users of discussion forums and social networking sites. This is where the real information is traded. A give-and-take on *Facebook* is so much more informative, and so much more authoritative, than anything provided by an official university web page.

Once they discover the extent of their cluelessness, some university bureaucrats, just as the ones at the LSE, respond with instinctive repression. They try to silence the professors and censor the students. Unable to side with the thinkers they join the thought police. This is when the bloggers have them cornered. The bureaucrats have scored an own goal. 'How can a university be in the business of restricting the freedom of speech? What are you afraid of anyway, you hypocrites?'

Blogging professors

Academics are by definition people who like to express themselves. They are also invariably vain. They crave an audience – students who sit at their feet and readers who snap up their tomes as soon as they hit the bookstores. Prestige, not money, is what really turns a professor on. Yet, since students don't sit at anyone's feet much any more, and since most academic books sell less than 500 copies, all professors are convinced that they are under-appreciated. The situation has become worse in recent years with the increasing pressure to publish. Major journals and prestigious university presses only accept a fraction of all submissions. What are all these expressive yet sadly misunderstood professors to do? Of course – they start blogging.

Many of the most famous bloggers are indeed professors. Professors Richard Posner and Gary Becker, U of Chicago, have a joint blog where they peddle their particular brand of free-wheeling conservatism. Brad Delong, econ prof at UC Berkeley, uses his *Semi-Daily Journal* to teach reality-based economics to libertarians and neoconservatives. Juan Cole, U of Michigan, writes an *Informed Comment* blog about the disaster which is Bush's Middle East policy. Norman Geras, a retired Marxist political science professor from Manchester, uses his *Normblog* to support the Iraq War and assorted leftist causes. Ed Felten, computer science professor at Princeton, and Lawrence Lessig, law professor at Standford, both use their blogs to defend the rights of users of technology and digitalized information. And this is just a small portion of the A-list of blogging profs.

Professors, being what they are, have been quick to attach theoretical significance to the blogging phenomenon. Richard Posner and Gary Becker insist that blogs exemplify the Austrian economist Friedrich Hayek's thesis that 'knowledge is widely distributed among people and that the challenge to society is to create mechanisms for pooling that knowledge'. Cass Sunstein, of NYU Law, is less sanguine. Hayek rules OK, he agrees, but blogs are often 'glib, superficial and irresponsible'. Others see blogging as the final realization of Jürgen Habermas' 'ideal speech situation', or perhaps as the long-delayed realization of Marshall McLuhan's idea of a 'global village'. To a lapsed academic like Timothy Leary, the internet was better than even LSD.

For universities blogging professors mean publicity. The professors strut their stuff online and bring glory to the institutions they work for. The fact that blogs still predominantly is a youthful medium means that they can be used to communicate directly with the universities' main audience – students, be they current, prospective or recent graduates.

Unfortunately, professors are often difficult to control. You never quite know quite where they are coming from and where they are going. Many professors are eccentrics, others are extremists. After all universities, together with mental asylums and prisons, are the three institutions where societies lock up their misfits.

Yet self-confident universities don't mind. And they shouldn't. A bit of controversy, even madness, is good PR. It generates a sense of excitement and intellectual daredevilry. There is nothing that students like more than a sense of excitement and intellectual daredevilry.

While most professors set up their own pages, there are universities that provide dedicated blogging sites which they encourage staff to use. Warwick University in the UK has a site, *Warwickblogs*, with 4,456 separate blogs and well over 80,000 entries. Harvard Law School also has a blogging service, *Weblogs at Harvard Law*, with hundreds of individual sites.

As some professors have discovered, blogs can help their teaching by allowing them to keep in closer contact with students. Blogs simplify collaborative projects, monitoring and support. Students can maintain course-specific blogs where they can develop their thoughts online. This is obviously ideal for a creative writing class but almost as promising for a course in political science, neurology or Renaissance art.

In addition, blogs provide exciting ways to conduct research. Why keep your research notes hidden in a drawer when you can put them online? This way you don't have to drag them around from one library to another. This way others also get access to them, to give comments, critique or praise. Blogs break the isolation of the lonely researcher, hook you up with others working on the same subject and help promote your work. As C Wright Mills explained:

> By keeping an adequate blog and thus developing self-reflective habits, you learn how to keep your inner world awake. Whenever you feel strongly about events or ideas you must try not to let them pass from your mind, but instead to formulate them on your blog and in so doing draw out their implications, show yourself either how foolish these feelings or ideas are, or how they might be articulated into productive shape.

No, Mills didn't write about blogs. He died in 1962, in the age of print media. You have to search the word 'blog' in the quote above and replace it with 'journal'. Still, the argument applies with the same force.

Let's put this point more strongly. There can be no such thing as secret research. For truth to prevail over falsehood every single step in the research process, from hypothesis to final conclusion, must be open to inspection. This is not an option, it's an obligation. In the olden days you were supposed to deposit your sources in an archive. Today you must put them on the web.

Aubrey Blumsohn, a senior lecturer in bone metabolism at the University of Sheffield, can tell you about the importance of openness. On a grant from Procter & Gamble, the American pharmaceutical giant, he was asked to sign his name to articles ghost-written by the company. A strange practice, one would have thought, especially since Blumsohn wasn't allowed to look at the data the articles relied on. When he brought the issue up with his employer he was reminded that Procter & Gamble sponsored much of University of Sheffield's research. Not prone to silence, Blumsohn blew the whistle on the shady business and was promptly suspended. In December 2005, the University of Sheffield offered him 120,000 pounds in return for a promise not to make any more 'detrimental or derogatory statements'. Refusing their offer, Blumsohn is now writing about it all in his *Scientific Misconduct* blog.

Blogging students

Students take to the internet like drinkers take to pubs. The web allows them to explore what the world of adult life has to offer but above all it allows them to socialize. To stay in contact with old friends, to make new ones, to network, cyber-stalk, flirt and tease. The web, in sharp contrast to their campus existence, is informal, low-pressure, irreverent and fun. Not surprisingly, students often have more of a presence online than they have in their classrooms.

Many students have their own blogs of course, but blogs are only part of the story. Often bloggers are regarded as pretty lonely and pretentious characters. And blog entries are uncomfortably similar to a professor's lecture. If nothing else, students tend to be weary of university-provided blogging sites. Why trust your university to provide you with a site when it's so easy to set one up for yourself?

In order to break out of the isolation of your blog many students rely on more social media – bulletin boards, chat rooms, discussion forums, and networking sites like *Facebook* and *MySpace*. Here, the lecture format is replaced by often raucous conversations. Instead of holding forth, people are hanging out. But, since they often can be combined, there is no absolute difference between blogs and these other more social formats.

The best example is *Facebook*. This is a website where you present a profile of yourself, together with photos, lists of interests, whatever comments you want to add, and extracts from your blog. You then go hunting for friends and for groups to hook yourself up with. Once you're connected, it is easy to communicate back and forth across your network and to expand it to include more nodes. It's more inviting than blogging, less intrusive than chats, and less exposed to spam than email.

What's truly amazing is *Facebook*'s saturation rate. Started by the Harvard student Mark Zuckerberg in February 2004, he had half of Harvard undergrads signed up within weeks. And from there, *Facebook* went on to conquer the world. In the US some 85 per cent of college students use it, there are 11 million users worldwide, and 20,000 new accounts are created every day. In 2006, it was the seventh most visited website and the world's largest site for photo sharing. Some 60 per cent of students log in daily and over 90 per cent log in once a week. According to a survey conducted by Student Monitor, a market researcher, students regard *Facebook* as the second coolest thing after iPods.

So what's so cool about it? It's simple. *Facebook* hooks you up. If you're looking for people who share your political opinions, or your sexual proclivities, you'll find them on *Facebook*. If you're curious whether that hunky guy at the back of the classroom is in a relationship, check out his profile. Want his cell phone number? Of course, it's in his profile too. It's all terribly addictive. As the *Urban Dictionary* warns, *Facebook* causes 'procrastination, swollen fingers, dropped grades, irritation of the eyes, increased need to add more friends to your friends list, and skipped classes.' Compare expressions like 'It's been 3 hours since I facebooked - I'm having withdrawls!' or a term like '*Facebook* slut' – 'A person who spends an inordinate amount of time on facebook.com, consistently adding people they don't know as friends, joining groups, stalking people.'

The funny thing is that university professors know so little about *Facebook* and next to no one uses it themselves. *Facebook* is a party organized by kids while the parents are away. The LSE in London, where I worked, had some 11,000 current and former students registered in the network, but no full-time academics. Not a single one. The professors actually believe that students are taking notes on their laptops during lectures. What they don't realize is that the students are all facebooking each other.

The thought police vs the professors

All in all, blogs and related internet use serve students and professors very well. It's empowering, pedagogically innovative, research-facilitating and it just might get you laid. What could be better? Yet, there are snakes in the garden. Trailing right after the thought comes the thought police.

One example are neocon websites that encourage students to rat on their teachers. Not ready to accept that people generally become more left-leaning as they acquire more education, these right-wing groups rely on reports from students to draw up lists of left-leaning profs. Some groups even pay students for their denunciations. Presumably the idea is to take the lists to the university's alumni and ask them to exercise pressure to have the pinkos removed.

In general, such tactics is not going to work. Individual professors have certainly come under fire but universities resent outside meddling and are loath to be seen to give in to it. Besides, getting rid of a tenured professor is a complex business. As far as freedom of speech is concerned, it is not the outsiders who create the problem. Instead, for professors and students alike, it is the university bureaucrats who pose the gravest threat.

In the autumn of 2004, a phantom began stalking the corridors of Southern Methodist University, SMU, in Dallas, Texas. She – yes it was clear it was a she – revealed herself exclusively through a blog, *The Phantom Professor*, in which some unpalatable truths about university life were spoken. Although SMU never was mentioned by name, administrators at the Department of Corporate Communications and Public Affairs thought they recognized themselves. Eventually, she was caught and revealed to be one Elaine Liner, a popular writing instructor and untenured SMU professor. Admitting to her crimes she was promptly informed that her contract would not be renewed at the end of the spring semester of 2005.

Yet, according to the SMU administrators, the blog was not the reason she was fired. Liner's services were simply no longer needed. At the same time they acknowledged that the content of her blog had bothered them. Among the posts there are plenty of digs at university bureaucrats and at Liner's more securely established colleagues. As an adjunct professor, says Liner, 'I felt like a phantom floating around campus.' The blog was her attempt to make sense of this disembodied existence. Seeing without being seen, she reported from faculty meetings, writing workshops, lectures and extracurricular activities. It is hard-hitting stuff although none of the targets are identified, nor indeed identifiable. It's also very funny and well observed. She must have been a great writing instructor.

The real problem was the *Phantom Professor*'s jaded view of a particular type of SMU student. She called them 'Ashleys' – the blonde, bitchy girls of privileged background, with their attention deficits, Gucci handbags, drug habits and bulimia. It is clear the descriptions are composites of many individuals, and there is also some considerable empathy with their privileged plight. But this was not good enough for SMU's literal-minded bureaucrats. They had received complaints, they said, and they were concerned that the blog was upsetting to some students and undermining their privacy. We support freedom of expression, they insisted, but we cannot allow students to get hurt. Of course the Ashleys felt singled out. They are after all next to identical copies of each other.

Meg Spohn has a similar story to tell. In December 2005, she was fired from DeVry University in Westminster, Colorado. 'I got called into the Academic Dean's office late Monday morning', she recounts the experience. 'The Human Resources person said they had become aware of my blog, and that I had made disparaging comments about DeVry and about its students on the blog, and that because of that, I was being let go.' Meg was escorted to her office, asked to pack up her things and taken to her car. There was no warning, no disciplinary procedure, discussion, or any process of notification or appeal.

Which precise blog entries stirred the ire of Meg Spohn's university remains obscure. However, DeVry does have a policy which states that staff cannot put anything in personal blogs that could hurt the university's stock prices. 'DeVry', prospective bloggers are reminded already in the first paragraph, 'is a publicly traded company'.

In any case her blog is only incidentally about DeVry. The occasional work references are mixed with references to everything else that makes up a life – reminiscences and anecdotes, thoughts on TV shows, love, lust and men. What the university got so upset about was nothing more than your average water-cooler bitching. Meg complained aloud when told how to grade her students, when DeVry hired practitioners instead of teachers, when the paperwork piled up. Is it really possible to be fired for complaining about paperwork? Yes, apparently, in the age of the internet, and at a university like DeVry.

The legality of the university's action can certainly be questioned and perhaps a good lawyer could have squeezed some money out of this publicly traded company. But after all the commotion Meg was not in the mood for a protracted legal wrangle. She got a new job and moved on with her life.

There are several other cases:

- In 2001, Duke University in Durham, North Carolina, shut down the website of Professor Gary Hull after he posted an article entitled 'Terrorism and Its Appeasement' that called for a bomb-the-hell-outa-them response to the 9/11 attacks on New York. Eventually, Duke reinstated Hull's web page but required him to add a disclaimer to the effect that the views expressed in the article did not reflect the views of the university.
- Leigh Blackall was fired from his job at the Educational Development Center of the University of Western Sydney, Australia, in 2005. As his managers explained, it was not for anything specific that he had written but because his blog constituted a risk to the university. His crime was to have discussed the disadvantages of the educational software the university was using. After contacting the union, he got six weeks' paid leave.
- In the spring of 2006, Bill Hobbs, a conservative pundit and 'blogging coach' at Belmont University, Nashville, Tennessee, was fired for publishing his own home-made version of those offensive, anti-Muhammad, Danish cartoons.
- In 2004, Amy Norah Burch, an undergraduate coordinator for the Committee on Degrees in Social Studies, was fired from Harvard University for the content of her blog. In one offensive entry she declared herself 'ready to get a shotgun and declare open season on all

senior faculty members and students who dared cross [her]'. And she was no doubt foolish to identify her 'anal retentive' boss by name.

• In June 2007, the pharmacologist David Colquhoun, one of the UK's leading scientists, was asked by the University College London, UCL, where he works, to remove parts of his blog from the university's server. Apparently disgruntled 'alternative therapists' had complained of his use of the word 'gobbledygook' in relation to some of their activities. Threatening legal action, the university authorities buckled. Remarkably, the UCL – home of Charles Darwin and Jeremy Bentham – censored one of its professors for publicly standing up in defence of science.

The conclusion which Meg Spohn draws from her ordeal apply to all these cases:

Yeah, I lost a job because of my blog, but it wasn't because I did anything wrong, was short-sighted or used flawed logic. It was because the institution I was working for violated my right to freedom of expression. …The lesson is not, 'Hey, you should be afraid to blog because of what might happen to your career.' The lesson is, 'Don't work for somebody who thinks it's okay to fire people for their thoughts.'

The thought police vs students

University administrators are giving students at some universities an equally hard time. Consider the case of the *Take Back Our Campus*, TBOC, blog started at Saint Lawrence University, New York, in the winter of 2004. The TBOC was a mixture of satire, made-up scoops and assorted embarrassing facts about students and faculty members. The posts were written anonymously, yet their seriousness of purpose was not in doubt: 'There is a battle raging on America's campuses', begins the first entry. 'Too many good students and professors at St Lawrence have been harassed, intimidated, and kicked around by prominent right-wing students and organizations, while prominent "liberal" students, organizations and administrators lay down on their spineless, turncoat backs.'

The campus Republicans were TBOC's primary target, together with what the blog claimed were their friends in the university administration. In one post a Republican student rep was identified by name as a cocaine user; there were suggestions that the university was covering up sexual violence on campus; and the blog complained about the undemocratic methods of electing the student council. In one entry a faculty member was lampooned for writing bad detective stories while ignoring his research, in another a faculty member was outed for his support of the South African apartheid regime. A tongue-in-cheek post identified the Dean of Student Affairs as a drug smuggler and member of Al Qaeda. 'Feel like you're being harassed?' the blog asked. 'That's probably because you're a whiney fuckwit suffering from the utter frustration of an uncomfortable confrontation that Mom and Dad's (but mostly Dad's) money can't solve.'

This was when the university reacted. The bloggers had to be stopped. This being the US of A, a lawsuit was quickly put together. But how do you sue someone whose identity is unknown? And what would you sue them for? The bloggers insisted they had evidence to back up all their factual claims and that no one surely could take the non-factual claims seriously. Taunting the administrators the bloggers offered to reveal their identities if the university only donated more money to students on financial aid. When the bloggers threatened to counter-sue, the university dropped their case. Yet TBOC's chief writer decided he had had enough and the blog was abandoned in October 2005. The university administrators and the on-campus Republicans must be sleeping much better these days.

Meanwhile, the thought police at University of California, Santa Barbara, UCSB, remains alert. *The Dark Side of UCSB* is a blog 'supported by students, former students and parents'. Its mission is to describe the 'deviant behaviours' of university students, including stories about crime, sexual assaults, excessive drinking and drug-taking. *The Dark Side* reports from the 'UCSB Fuck Fest', recites the latest campus crime statistics and complains about noise and disorderliness.

The university objected to these descriptions and its lawyers decided that use of the 'UCSB' acronym in the blog's name was an infringement on the university's trademark. Yet getting their own lawyers on-board, it was easy for *The Dark Side* to show that the university's threats violated their constitutional right to free speech. Despite the UCSB having dropped the case in early 2005, it continues to insist that the blog 'defames' the university. *The Dark Side* is defiantly blogging away. Most recently it blogged about a UCSB student killing another in a drunken driving accident.

As one would expect given their informality, social networking sites have gotten students into no end of trouble. On *Facebook* it's easy to slag your university off. Check out groups like 'Yale Sucks', 'Harvard Schmarvard', 'Columbia is a better school than NYU', or 'People Who Got into Stanford Grad School and Didn't Go'.

The problem is only that the university administrators too may be reading. College authorities are reported to monitor websites looking for parties they can raid and on-campus drug pushers they can arrest. As a result *Facebook* has become the new front line in the battle for on-campus free speech. Here are a few recent cases:

- In September 2005, the University of Central Florida tried to prosecute a student for 'harassment' after he created a *Facebook* group where he called a student representative 'a jerk and a fool'.
- At Cowley College, Kansas, the university reacted after students posted complaints about the teaching in the Theatre Department.

- At University of Syracuse, New York, the administrators objected to 'vulgar comments' about a teaching assistant in a *Facebook* group.

Facebook presents challenges for college athletes, and for some reason female soccer players seem to be particularly vulnerable. At San Diego State University, California, four members of the women's soccer team were suspended since they posted bawdy pictures of their post-match shenanigans. Northwestern suspended its entire women's soccer team after similar pictures ended up on a website called *BadJocks.com*.

To prevent such problems some universities have instituted blanket bans. At Loyola University in Chicago athletes are banned from using *Facebook* and violating the policy could cost them their scholarships. The state universities of Utah and Colorado have banned social networking sites on computers in their athletics departments. There are no similar policies for general students. Yet, the thought police themselves willingly confess to their befuddlement – 'The administration can't tell you exactly how to deal with it because there's no handbook on it', says a coach at San Diego State University, interviewed in the local newspaper. 'I'm just trying to figure out how to Google, for crying out loud.'

This policy is obviously outrageous. To ban jocks from using *Facebook* is like banning them from chewing tobacco or receiving blow jobs by busty blondes.

Are universities different?

A pretty clear pattern emerges from these cases. The greatest threat against freedom of speech on the internet comes from the very people responsible for running the university. They are the ones who put in long hours compiling evidence against bloggers, taking notes and backing up web pages on their hard disks.

If anything this shows how far removed the university's bosses are from the academic life of the universities they are in charge of. University bureaucrats rarely have higher degrees. They don't have a commitment to critical inquiry and independence of thought. Let's face it, they just aren't that bright. Today's university executives are the very same people the professors gave B minuses to back when they were students. Clearly, they don't understand what a university is and what it's supposed to be.

University bosses for their part, have just as much disdain for academics. Professors are lazy, they wear rumpled suits, they don't come in on time in the morning. Universities, the bureaucrats believe, would be far better off without the academics. In fact, they would be far better off without students too. Without students and professors the bureaucrats could just send off university diplomas to whoever is prepared to pay for them.

But not all universities are as bad. Not all universities use repressive tactics. The notorious cases concern, shall we say, less than prestigious universities in less than central locations. It's Southern Methodist University and the University of Western Sydney, not Stanford, Princeton or Yale. Or they concern places like DeVry which isn't a proper university at all but rather a profit-making corporation with degrees as its business idea. The few cases that don't fit this pattern – Harvard and Duke – can probably best be explained through idiosyncratic factors: a particularly nasty supervisor and the jittery emotions of post-9/11 America.

Moreover, the people who get censored are themselves always marginal – non-tenured faculty members, teachers on temporary contracts, or students working off their scholarships in the university administration. These are people who are vulnerable and easy to scare. If you're tenured, or if your father is a famous alum, you have far more protection.

There is a risk of self-censorship here. It may indeed be stupid for non-tenured faculty to start blogging, at least if your politics diverges from that of the *monstres sacrés* of your department.

Maybe promotion will be slower or you'll get more paperwork to do. Or if you can't control the urge, maybe you'd better start blogging anonymously. Maybe students should shut up too, at least if they work in a university office between their classes.

The risk of self-censorship and anonymization demonstrate the importance of having a policy on blogging and related internet use. It's not fair to judge students and staff in secret, based on non-existent laws, arbitrarily interpreted by people who know little about the intellectual life of the universities they pretend to run. Justice, just as much as truth, requires publicity and a due process.

The UK breaks with this pattern. Here well-established universities have been known to go after well-established academics. Whatever you say about the London School of Economics or the University College London, they are not some for-profit, faith-based universities somewhere on the American prairie. Why are institutions of this calibre so scared of free speech? The answer is of course that a university education is big business. In a situation where the government is cutting funding, the universities become increasingly dependent on student fees. They have bills to pay, targets to reach and quotas to fill. When a university education is sold like so many sausages, no bloggers are allowed to stand in the way. And no principles.

This is also why a university like the University of California, Santa Barbara, reacted so strongly to complaints about the raunchy extracurricular activities of its students. Sex, drugs and rock 'n roll is of course exactly what students are looking for, but it's not what most parents want to subsidize. This is also why some US universities have cracked down hard on internet use by college athletes. College athletes are supposed to be role models and spokespersons for their schools. The real goings-on in locker rooms and at post-game parties were always widely known but they were rarely talked about. At least not in public.

The truth is of course that universities indeed are very differ-ent. A university education is not a sausage factory. Universities should foster critical inquiry, not stifle it. Encourage freedom of speech, not repress it. Universities are nothing like a company. A company that stifles and represses is just a regular company, but a university that stifles and represses is not a university any more.

Some universities seem to have an intuitive understanding of this issue. The University of Warwick, which has a large university-run blogging site, also has a liberal policy on matters of free speech. Said the person in charge of the site:

> I wouldn't say that we have rules which are specifically about what people can and can't say about the university. Indeed our blogs frequently contain robust criticism of aspects of the institution and broadly we welcome that; understanding our staff and students' concerns, doubts and worries about the institution is important to us, as is the idea that we are not afraid of criticism, as is the idea that we support freedom of speech.

The anxious university administrators are quite simply wrong. Discordant voices, intellectual controversy and a bit of cheek is just what students want. This is what a university education is about and this is why they show up for classes. At large, famous and self-confident universities have realized this a long time ago. They know repression is likely to backfire and that a university's reputation for supporting freedom of speech is one of its most important assets.

5
Bloggers @ Work

Let's say a bit more about companies. Business corporations have two main constituencies. Inside the companies there are employees and outside the companies there are customers. Business corporations exercise power over both. They make their employees work as hard as they can, while paying them as little as possible. And they convince customers to pay top dollars for goods that are as cheaply put together as they can get away with.

Companies benefit enormously from the fact that employees and customers are dispersed and usually utterly disorganized. Workers, on the whole, don't join trade unions, and customers, on the whole, don't fight for their rights. Both groups find it costly to use their voices – it takes time to go to meetings, to sign petitions, and it is not clear what such activism can achieve anyway. Instead of voicing their complaints, they simply exit. Employees find better jobs elsewhere and consumers scour the market looking for cheaper deals. Companies, as a result, get away with too much.

Blogs can alter this imbalance of power, at least to some extent. On the internet, the cost of using one's voice has gone way down and even dispersed people can be virtually united. You go to websites instead of meetings and leave comments in discussion forums instead of signing petitions. And of course, everyone has their own blog. In the blogosphere, workers and consumers are less likely to simply exit and more likely to stand up and fight for their rights.

And even those who prefer to exit will benefit from the information the internet provides. Before joining a certain company, you surf the web to find out what bloggers say about it, how much they pay and how they treat the staff. Or, before committing yourself to a certain purchase, you read the online reviews. Information like this counteracts corporate misinformation and advertising hype. It improves your bargaining position and makes it possible to make better choices. More information, as always, is empowering.

Of course the companies hate it. 'Bloggers are spreading false rumours and ruining our businesses', screamed a feature article in *Forbes Magazine* in November 2005. 'It's just not fair!' And of course the blogosphere may contain falsehoods, but the companies hate it just as much when the information is correct. The world should not be told what a particular boss really is like or how many toilet breaks the staff are allowed per shift. Blogging about such matters is to 'bring the company into disrepute', and it may get the author disciplined or even fired. Is this really legal? Maybe, maybe not. Is it a dirty, misconceived, tactic likely to backfire? Most certainly. But in all probability, the bloggers will have the last laugh.

Cybergriping

I recently sent 20 boxes with family memorabilia to Sweden as part of a complicated transcontinental house-move. I made the mistake of relying on DHL. The boxes were supposed to arrive in three days but three weeks later no one had any idea where they were. I spent hours on the phone talking to various, and increasingly uninterested, DHL representatives. DHL in England blamed DHL in Sweden, and DHL in Sweden blamed ... yes, they blamed DHL in England.

In the end I had had enough and started blogging about it. I even smuggled a link into the 'DHL' article in *Wikipedia* and my blog was getting hundreds of DHL-related hits per day before the lexicographers caught up with me. No, it probably wasn't a fair description of what indeed may be a wonderfully efficient company. But the story was true and I was very upset at the time. In the end 19 boxes arrived, but without an apology or a refund of my additional expenses. I still occasionally find myself wondering what happened to the twentieth box ...

We all have our DHL experiences and bloggers around the world are reacting to them in much the same way. A company fails to deliver something on time, repair something properly, or some item you buy turns out to be faulty or incomplete. Phone calls to the company take you to call centres in India or Glasgow where overworked operatives read out to you from pre-prepared scripts in a hard-to-follow accent. In the past you had to grit your teeth and bear it. Today, you write about it in your blog.

It's known as 'cybergriping', the act, that is, of 'complaining about a company, its goods or services, in a blog or a website'. And a blog or website that is devoted to griping about a particular company is known as a 'gripe site'.

Gripe sites provide a great outlet for the mis-sold and disserviced. If there is real discontent out there, the site will pick it up, articulate and magnify it. Before long a community of discontent is created around the blog, with people leaving comments and swapping horror stories. The bigger the site, the easier it is for search-engines to find and soon it will pop up next to the big company itself in a Google search. Prospective customers looking for information will see the comments and before long they may not be prospective customers any more. Baffled PR types wonder how their multimillion dollar marketing efforts suddenly was subverted by a single disgruntled guy with a web page. The damage to the company could be very substantial indeed. And serves them right too.

Streamlinenet is a UK-based company that provides internet hosting, space for personal web pages. *Streamlinenet*'s image is that of a cheap, cheerful company which gives a no-frills service at a rock-bottom price. The price is indeed low but in the view of some customers the company's level of service is even lower. And, tellingly, *Streamlinenet* is not cheerful. Not cheerful at all.

As one would expect, many of the disaffected customers are bloggers. *Streamlinenet*, they claim, take far too long to deal with their complaints. Replies, when they arrive, are often bizarre and seem automatically generated. *Streamlinenet* is also alleged to be heavy-handed in censoring material. One user put a picture of a 'penisaurus' on his blog – a photo of a public toilet wall, hardly hard-core porn – and soon his entire account was deleted. Getting more personal, a former employee claims that *Streamlinenet* charged money for things they never delivered, and continued to bill credit cards long after customers had cancelled their services. *Streamlinenet*'s owner was called things never mentioned in the company's prospectus – crook, jerk, low-life scum.

Interestingly, *Streamlinenet* didn't passively accept the flack. They fought back. They contacted an internet site where various web hosts were reviewed and demanded they take down posts that were critical of them. They contacted *Blogger*, the largest Google-owned blog host, and asked that they take action against a blogger with strong anti-*Streamlinenet* views. In both cases, the official claim was that the customers had infringed on *Streamlinenet*'s copyright by quoting extensively from the company's emails. About the same time a number of highly positive, 10/10, reviews of *Streamlinenet*'s services started appearing on various review sites. Was this just a coincidence? The dissatisfied customers clearly didn't think so. They were convinced the reviews were planted by the company.

Some of these threats clearly had an effect. Some blog entries seem to have been deleted or otherwise altered. Still, much criticism of the company remains. An entry entitled 'Avoid *Streamlinenet*' appears right underneath the official *Streamlinenet* entry in a simple Google search. Of course it must affect their business negatively.

You may feel that this is unfair. Perfectly decent and hard-working companies may suffer as a result of stories spread by a few disgruntled bloggers. Some stories may be true but others may not be. Prospective customers suspecting fire where there is smoke, are likely to run away. Still, web-surfers are surely more sophisticated judges of information than nervous business execs assume. We all know people who like to complain about things. The fact that these people now have websites makes them no more trustworthy.

Surely we should be far more upset about the wrongs which the bloggers are trying to set right – the continuous lies, half-truths, and deceptions spread by companies regarding the quality of their products. We are used to companies lying for the sake of profits, but lying for the sake of profits doesn't excuse the crime. It aggravates it.

Yet the story has a reasonably happy conclusion. *Streamlinenet* seems to have realized that legal threats isn't going to work and that they have to improve their services. The company has gotten better. They pay more attention to customer complaints these days and have laid off some of the heavy-handed tactics. Most of the critics have gone silent. Perhaps, *Streamlinenet* should have listened more to the bloggers in the first place?

The corporate flog

A more clever way for companies to get back at bloggers is to impersonate them. Companies too after all can start blogging. Blogs are potentially a great way to market things. They are cheap, they reach an enormous online market, and they speak to customers in new ways. In an age when most people are very cynical about glossy corporate propaganda, the irreverence of a cheeky little blog can easily help re-brand a product and a company.

Wal-Mart, the American retail giant, is famous not only for its low prices but also for its low wages and the repressiveness of its corporate culture. Wal-Mart has been suffering an image problem lately, as disgruntled employees set up support groups on the web. The internet is positively buzzing with often angry, anti-Wal-Mart propaganda. Trying to improve on its image, Wal-Mart too, took to blogging.

Well no, they didn't actually. Rather, their PR firm, a company called Edelman, did. Or to be precise, a lobby group Edelman set up, 'Working Families for Wal-Mart', sponsored the trip of an 'ordinary American couple' – Laura and Jim – to one Wal-Mart store after another across the US. In each new place they talked to local employees and blogged about their impressions. As they discovered, employees were invariably very satisfied with their jobs and Wal-Mart invariably contributed greatly to the local community. Yeah, right.

When the hoax was revealed there was embarrassment all around. The blogosphere was scathing and quickly unearthed other attempts by Edelman to pay bloggers for positive write-ups. But the bloggers were at the same time very smug to have their new powers acknowledged by such a well-known company. Blogs, Wal-Mart's clumsy efforts confirmed, can achieve what no official marketing can do.

Differently put, blogs are great for creating, maintaining and improving corporate identities. A company with a gutsy blog is no longer a cold multinational behemoth. Overnight it becomes a friend, someone you know and like and trust. Or a company might set up a website like McDonald's *Open for Discussion* blog which aims to 'create a forum for increased dialogue and engagement'. How could companies that blog with such noble aims ever underpay their workers? Or for that matter, dump industrial waste in poor countries or oil rigs in Arctic waters?

The problem is only how to convincingly pull this off. Let's face it, irony and cheekiness don't come naturally to multinational corporations, and most invitations to 'dialogue' sound patently insincere. An obvious solution is for the company's PR people to take charge of the re-branding exercise, but often this proves difficult. After all, PR people are paid to present the official image, not the unofficial. They know about press releases but they don't have the authority to start chatting away, informally, about this and that and the other.

The only person who can blog convincingly is probably the boss, the CEO or the company's owner. No one else can be self-deprecating without getting into trouble. If the company is lucky they have a boss with a knack for turning a phrase, and there are indeed some celebrated examples of blogging CEOs. The head of one of France's biggest supermarket chains, Michel Edouard Leclerc, has a blog in which he discusses his business, his love of food and good literature. The bosses at General Motors have a *Fast Lane* blog where they discuss the latest car designs and their aversion to laws on fuel emissions. The Boeing bosses have blogs too and lots and lots of execs at computer companies do – Sun Microsystems, Hewlett-Packard, IBM and Hitachi.

The problem is only that blogging takes time and most CEOs will be far too busy. Most are also likely to be insufficiently literate or constitutionally incapable of diverging from the corporate hype. One possible solution is to have a ghost-writer put the blog together. There is a booming industry in ghost-writing services on offer to corporate clients. There are also plenty of self-styled 'consultants' who advice companies on how to let their hair down online.

The latent silliness of these ventures should be obvious. In most cases blogging corporations are stern faces wearing grinning masks designed by hired hacks. Depending on the skills of the operators involved and the gullibility of the web-surfing readership, it just might work. Yet many flogs, like the pro-Wal-Mart stunt, teeter on the brink of a PR disaster.

Getting dooced

Yet the really interesting cases concern employees. People who work for a company always have a lot of juicy stuff to tell – tales of mistakes and mismanagement, gossip and intrigues. But employees also have a lot at stake. They are dependent on the companies they work for – for a salary, a career and a social life. The companies have considerable power over them. In the past, this power was exercised in order to make sure that no unfavourable stories escaped the office or the factory gates. Managing a company was all about manipulating information and shutting people up. In today's blog-saturated environment, this is far more difficult to do.

The blogging phenomenon first appeared at a time when the very notion of work was undergoing dramatic changes, above all in the US. It used to be that people stayed with the same company for years. You were socialized into the company's way of thinking and you were loyal to your employer much as you were loyal to your spouse. And as a valuable and trusted worker, and as a quasi-family member, the company was loyal to you. This was the traditional contract which united companies and staff.

But this world is now all but gone. The traditional contract has been torn up. Today, labour is more often than not considered as just another factor of production the cost of which should be minimized. This is why companies are downsizing, outsourcing, firing and then re-hiring the same people on renegotiated and inferior terms.

In this new, and far more insecure environment, employees aren't loyal in the same way as previously. Only the exceedingly slow-witted will trust an employer who is likely to fire them at a moment's notice. Since their loyalty no longer can be taken for granted, employees must instead be controlled through other means. This is why corporate practices in recent years have become increasingly repressive. Computerized technology has provided unprecedented ways of policing staff. Email and web use are monitored, and keystrokes on computers are routinely recorded. As American companies in particular have come to realize, scared workers bring in higher profits than happy workers.

But computers are not only enslaving employees but also helping liberate them. Employees are turning to the web for emotional sustenance and support. You blog in order to make friends, deal with stress, with unreasonable bosses or difficult colleagues. You blog to sound off or take the piss and you blog to subvert a corporate image which presents you as an ever-smiling manikin. You blog to stay sane. You blog to stay human.

How the bosses react to such insubordination is easy to imagine. They get upset, they get mad, they reach for the corporate rulebook. In many cases bloggers have been dooced. To be 'dooced' is to be 'fired from work because of things one has written in one's blog'. As in, 'Dude, I heard Janey got dooced last week.' Or 'I was dooced yesterday because some scumbag sent my boss the link to my blog.'

The term itself was coined by Heather B Armstrong in 2002 after she was sacked for writing about work and colleagues in her blog, 'Dooce.com'. Although she never identified herself by name, nor the company she worked for, her boss felt exposed to public ridicule. Heather's real crime, it seems is that she was wittier and more articulate than her boss. She was also unlucky to have colleagues without a sense of humour.

> Exercise your right not to shower, as practicing basic hygiene only makes their lives easier. You will look presentable when you want to look presentable, and today just isn't one of those days. Today is, however, the day the company's primary investor will be taking a tour of the new office. Think to yourself what a coincidence this is.

Although the terminology itself was new, Ms Armstrong was not the first person to be fired for blogging. This honour seems rightly to belong to Ian Lind, an investigative reporter with the *Star-Bulletin* in Honolulu, Hawaii. He was fired in 2001 for maintaining a blog in which the shady dealings of the proprietor of his paper were exposed to public view. As a journalist he was supposed to rake muck, but this was in-house muck and it stuck to his employer.

Since these first cases millions of people have taken up blogging and the number of people dooced, or 'star-bulletined', have multiplied rapidly. There are today a hundred plus cases.

Is it legal? Can companies really fire you for exercising your constitutional right to free speech? Basically this depends on the employment law in each respective country. American laws are the most favourable to employers and this explains the disproportionate amount of dooced Americans. In some American states – IT-friendly California for example – people are employed 'at will', meaning that they can be fired 'for good reason, bad reason, or no reason at all'. The slightest whiff of a blog-related problem and you are out the door.

On the other hand, there are also American states – in some cases the very same ones – where it is illegal to fire people who engage in legal activities in their own spare time. Engaging in an activity – free speech – which is protected by the First Amendment should consequently not be a cause for dismissal. This conflict has so far not been tested by the courts.

In Europe, on the whole, employees are far better protected, although people have been dooced both in Britain and in France. But again, there are many other ways short of a sacking in which your employer can make your life impossible. Intransigent bloggers are often bullied by bosses and by colleagues, but bullying is a crime which is notoriously difficult to prove in court.

Blowing whistles & spilling beans

There are broadly speaking four different reasons why bloggers are dooced: for blowing whistles, spilling beans, for being generally insubordinate and for undermining the company's image.

For a whistle-blower a blog is the perfect venue. A company does something morally questionable or outright illegal – they dump industrial waste, let's say, in a children's playground – and you happen to find out about it. The local newspaper is in cahoots with the company's owner and the police think you're insane. What do you do? In a Hollywood film from the 1950s the hero would have taken the issue to Washington, but today you write about it in your blog.

Spilling beans is different from whistle-blowing in that no moral issue motivates the blogger. To spill beans is to leak information which shouldn't have been made public. Perhaps the secret will benefit a competitor, a counterpart in a negotiation, or a tax inspector. Some such leaks may be intentional but others are mistakes. But even when there was no intention to do harm the company may decide that the person in question is a security risk.

Interestingly, the vast majority of dooced bean-spillers worked in internet-based companies. You'd expect internet companies to be blogger-friendly and used to the informal banter of the web. And all in all, they surely are. They are also heavily dependent on the right to freedom of speech. But this hasn't stopped them from cracking the whip.

In 2004, Joyce Park, aka Troutgirl, worked for *Friendster*, a social networking site. She was also a blogger and when *Friendster* made some changes to the software it used on its site, she discussed them in her blog. Some of these changes were controversial and Troutgirl's comments sparked quite a debate. Yet everything she said was publicly known, and when she was fired in August 2004, she was as taken aback as her readers. Her crime, it seems, was to have admitted that the *pros* of the software changes came with some *cons*.

In October 2003, Michael Hanscom published a photo on his blog which showed a crate of brand-new Apple computers being offloaded at Microsoft's headquarters in Seattle. 'It looks like somebody over in Microsoft land is getting some new toys', he wrote, and this was enough to get him dooced from his job with MSCopy, a print shop on Microsoft's campus.

Yet, Michael Hanscom didn't blame Microsoft. He believes a company should have the prerogative to fire an employee for such photographic indiscretions. Microsoft believed he presented a security risk and that was that. '*Mea culpa, mea culpa, mea maxima culpa.*' People commenting on his blog were not as charitable. 'Holy fucking shit, I can't believe they dismissed you for something so harmless.' 'Who's surprised that Microsoft buys Apple computers?'

Google is a company widely admired among web users. 'We have an unusually open organization', says a Google job ad, 'where communication is actively encouraged among all employees and business information is broadly disseminated'. Yet Mark Jen has a slightly different perspective. In January 2005, he moved to San Francisco to begin his new job with Google. Rather than repeating the same story 20 times over in emails back home to friends, he recorded his initial impressions in his blog.

Like any first day on any job his was a combination of excitement, confusion and boring presentations by people from Human Resources. But overall Mark was very enthusiastic. He got a great new laptop to take home; they threw a fun party with plenty of booze; the health care package was first class and he could use 20 per cent of company time to work on his own projects. Work was fun, and fun was work. And Google was constantly rolling out new products:

> both google's profits and revenue are growing at an unprecedented rate even while they are increasing their expenditures on capital and human resources, not to mention that google has been primarily focused on the US market and is now turning their full attention to the global marketplace; … if you guys thought gmail and google groups were cool, you ain't seen nothing yet!

His mum and friends back home in Michigan must have been happy to hear that he was doing so well. What Mark did not realize, however, was that the blogosphere is full of 'Google-watchers' who eagerly seize on any crumb of information that escapes from the search-engine empire. To Google-watchers his blog was hot stuff, and before he knew it Mark was getting tens of thousands of visitors per day.

This was when Google's executives got nervous. A particularly sensitive entry was the one quoted above. Mark had discussed Google's expected revenue stream; he had said it was 'growing at an unprecedented rate'. Not good! They called him in and asked him to remove the reference. He did and wrote about it – 'i goofed and put some stuff up on my blog that's not supposed to be there' – and happily went on blogging. But on 28 January, 11 days after beginning his new job, he was fired. They didn't mention the blog at the time, but Mark had no doubt that he had been dooced.

What's amazing about these accounts is the way the companies overreacted. The information Troutgirl discussed in her blog was already publicly available. Michael Hanscom's photos were as unremarkable as holiday snaps. Mark Jen's revelations were no proper revelations at all. Yet the companies pounced on them.

Why? Surely it's not a coincidence that these are web-based companies. As web-based companies they worry a lot about web-based information that might hurt relations with financial investors. In a world where the smallest unconfirmed rumours can move stock market prices, it's far better if everyone just shuts up. The problem is that freedom of speech in this way comes to be restricted by the very volatile movements of the stock market.

What's also amazing is the very apologetic attitude of the bloggers concerned. They don't blame the companies, they blame themselves. As though their constitutionally guaranteed rights mean nothing in comparison with the company's right to fire people at will.

Poking fun, grumbling & letting off steam

By far the most common reason why bloggers get fired is that they poke fun at their employers, grumble or let off steam.

Catherine Sanderson, known to her thousands of daily readers as *La Petite Anglaise*, is an English woman who, before her crimes were discovered, worked as a secretary for Dixon Wilson, an English accountancy firm in Paris. Her blog, begun in 2004, contained a predictable collection of ex-pat gripes about the French, but soon she started writing about more personal issues – her adoption, love affairs, the tribulations of single motherhood. Very occasionally *La Petite Anglaise* discussed work. Although she never revealed her real name, nor the name of her employer, some of the partners in the firm thought they recognized themselves. One day she posted a few photos of herself and this was the pretext they needed to pounce. The partners thought that the photos identified *La Petite Anglaise* to her readers and that they identified their company.

The entries themselves are funny, well observed and well written. It's gentle parody, no hard-hitting stuff. A senior partner is described as 'very old school' – a man who 'wears braces and sock suspenders, stays in gentlemen's clubs when in London and calls secretaries "typists."' 'When I speak to him', she writes, 'I can't prevent myself from mirroring his plummy Oxbridge accent'. There is another piece about a Christmas party where someone breaks the 'unwritten rule' of pulling his cracker before the senior partner and his wife have pulled theirs.

According to *La Petite Anglaise*, these were 'intended as humorous anecdotes, nothing more'. Dixon Wilson, however, saw it differently. According to her employer the entries gave them the 'right of dismissal with real and serious cause'. In addition, having gone through the blog with a fine tooth comb, they discovered that Catherine Sanderson had played hooky on no fewer than two occasions. She had called in sick but, as the blog revealed, she had actually gone off to see a lover.

The story ends well. *La Petite Anglaise* took Dixon Wilson to court. In France, a stipulation regarding loyalty to the employer is a part of standard employment contracts and the judges needed to decide whether the blog entries violated this clause. In March 2007, Catherine Sanderson won her case. She got a year's salary and court costs paid. Can anyone baby-sit tonight, she asked triumphantly in her blog, 'so I can go out and paint the town red?'

Another case is that of Joe Gordon, who was fired from Waterstone's bookshop in Edinburgh in January 2005 after working there for 11 years. Waterstone accused him of 'gross misconduct' and of 'bringing the company into disrepute'. His crime was to have maintained a blog, *The Woolamaloo Gazette*, in which he made very occasional, if less than perfectly flattering, references to his employer.

Yet, while reading the entries it is very difficult to find much objectionable material. Joe wrote about the books that crossed his desk and the thoughts that crossed his mind. There are observations about the weather, about the streets of Edinburgh, and assorted expressions of sexual anxiety. Joe Gordon was just being himself online.

Yes, there were bits and pieces about Waterstone's, although Joe never mentioned which particular branch he worked in. There is some whining and some grumbling – familiar stuff to anyone who ever had a job. Like Dixon Wilson, the detectives at Waterstone's had to sift through hundreds of entries and thousands of words before they got to a paragraph like this one for 16 November 2004:

Evil boss then has cheek to ask me to work one of the bloody bank holidays in the week he refused me off. Cheeky smegger. Said no. Noticing he has put me down for one of those days anyway, the sandal-wearing bastard. Words will be exchanged – if he gives me my birthday off I will do his bank holiday day. If not he can kiss my magnificent Celtic ass.

How many books on the shelves of Waterstone's contain similar outbursts? 'Gross misconduct?' 'Bringing into disrepute?' Waterstone's should have looked up the meaning of these words before they overreacted, but perhaps they couldn't find a dictionary? And don't forget: Waterstone's wouldn't be in business if people weren't allowed to think, write and publish freely. Their behaviour is enough to make you want to go and surf the Amazon.com website.

These examples can easily be multiplied. Bloggers are dooced left, right and centre.

- 'Mr Fabulous' was fired from Life South Community Blood Centers in Florida for talking about anal rape in a flippant way in his *Pointless Drivel* blog.
- Bill Poon in California got dooced from a burger joint when he posted a picture of his boss on *MySpace*. According to the boss this constituted 'identity theft' and was a criminal offence.
- Peter Whitney was dooced from Wells Fargo, a US bank, just as the PR Department launched an official company blog as a way to improve relations with its customers.
- Nadine Haobsh was fired from her job as beauty editor at the New York-based *Ladies Home Journal* once her blog revealed just how many freebie gifts fashion editors receive.
- Matt Donegan was dooced from Dover Post in Delaware for what his paper claimed were racist remarks.
- Kelly Kreth was dooced from Dwelling Quest, a real estate agent, for two negative posts about her employer – who wasn't even mentioned by name.
- Melissa Lafsky, the *Opinionista*, who wrote on the dehumanizing aspects of life in law firms, wasn't technically fired from Littler Mendelson, a New York law firm, rather she outed herself in her blog and then resigned.

- A marine biologist, Jessa Jeffries, was fired from the Philadelphia Museum where she worked since 'the tone, language and content' of her blog 'did not reflect the values of their institution'. Jessa, according to her bio, 'has bangs, wears dresses' and loves to do various things with slimy creatures. She looks good too.
- 'Donny B' was fired from a Chicago store for comments left on his blog by *one of his readers*.

Etc and so on.

Undermining the corporate image

Many jobs in today's service economy require employees to manufacture and sell emotions. Companies care for their customers and they want them to feel well looked after. Except that they don't of course. What companies really care about aren't customers but profits. In order to conceal this fact they employ people who genuinely care about customers. Except that employees don't care either. What they really care about aren't customers but salaries. The customers, for their part, know fully well that this is the case, but it's part of the make-believe of a service economy that they pretend not to notice.

As a result everyone has to act. The company, the employees and the customers are all buying and selling a product – 'service' – they know to be a fake. Yet the make-believe isn't that difficult for companies and customers to cope with. The company executives are far removed from the actual delivery of the service and the customers, perversely, are often flattered even by attention which is patently phony.

It is instead for the employees that play-acting presents the greatest challenge. Air stewardesses provide a famous example. These airborne dinner ladies have to deal with drunkards, gropers, screaming children, lost passengers and delayed planes while always and constantly smiling. They have to be sexually attractive but they can't be inviting; they must make promises which they constantly betray. Regardless of what they actually feel, they have to learn to cover up their emotions and then cover up for the fact that they are covering up.

It's enough to make you want to scream. It's enough to make you pour drinks into people's laps and attach the neckties of business-class passengers to overhead lockers. Or why not stab someone from Staff Development with one of those silly little plastic knives? Today such imagined revenges can easily become real. You can do it all, and more, in the virtual reality of your blog. You go on smiling at work while bitching ferociously online.

What companies make of this is easy to imagine. The secret collusion of audience and actor is shattered; the slip is showing together with the strings that attach the puppet to the puppeteer's hands. 'All our hard efforts and along comes some fool with a blog!'

Take the case of Ellen Simonetti, an air hostess who worked for Delta Airlines. In her *Queen of Sky* blog she kept a thinly veiled diary of things that happened at work – the ups and the downs with the trolley in the aisle. There are lots of photos, including snapshots of what 'crew members really do on layovers (especially in Spain)'. Everyone likes to read about the glamorous world of in-flight attendants and the blog was getting thousands of hits per day.

In October 2005, Simonetti was fired for what the company referred to as 'misuse of uniform'. Her crime was to have posted a few pictures of herself in a stewardess uniform, inside an empty airplane, showing just a bit too much cleavage and a bit too much leg. These were just hints, mind you, nothing actually undressed. But the message the pictures sent off differed in no uncertain ways from the official corporate. There was too much sexual promise and not enough denial. The *Queen of Sky* was obviously not taking her acting job seriously.

Not one to go quietly, Simonetti hired a law firm to pursue Delta Airlines for 'wrongful termination, defamation of character and lost future wages'. For a while she also relied on a PR company to handle all requests for interviews. The offensive photos were taken down for a while but were quickly uploaded again when her doocing hit the headlines.

Fighting back

Customers and employees used to be isolated and unorganized. Companies had power over them since they controlled access to information. Ignorance and isolation equalled powerlessness. This is still the case of course, and customers and employees are still at a disadvantage. But the internet has begun to redress the imbalance.

Interestingly, bloggers are always dooced for stepping on a company's most sensitive toes. In clunky old companies, British ones in particular, you get fired for insolence, for saying impertinent things about your boss and your colleagues. In internet-based companies they don't care about that sort of thing since they have made an art out of cheekiness. What really matters to them are instead share prices, and the accusation against bloggers is always that they give investors the hiccups. In companies whose main product is a carefully pedicured and coiffed image – airplane companies for example – bloggers get fired for any evidence that they aren't taking their thespian obligations seriously.

In all cases, the bloggers' real crime is to have subverted company's hierarchies. The power of the bosses always depended on their ability to depersonify their underlings, to treat them as faceless and voiceless fodder for their corporate plans. This, after all, is the logic of torturers everywhere. By giving faces and voices back to employees, blogs make such depersonalization far more difficult to engage in. The anonymous underlings have turned out to be human beings after all, with thoughts, dreams and lives which are distinctly their own. And in many cases the lives in question are considerably more interesting than the lives of the bosses themselves.

Imagine that your secretary starts a blog. She begins to write and before long she has 5,000 visitors a day. 'What?' you say. 'My secretary has 5,000 visitors a day!?' 'My fucking secretary has 5,000 fucking visitors per day! How dares she?' The blog has brought about a real shift in power between the two of you. Not only is your secretary speaking directly to more people than you ever will, but she commands their attention. She is popular and fun whereas you only are feared. Before long you start suspecting your house-cleaner of blogging, perhaps even your nanny. Curious and half-crazed you start surfing the web looking for them. Yes, there they are. They too have blogs, they too have lives. How can you ever forgive them?

Yet, repressive measures are not going to work. If nothing else the companies will find that repression is prohibitively costly. For censorship to operate smoothly, the companies need procedures for detecting bloggers, for monitoring and disciplining them and for dealing with whatever court cases that result. Consider, for example, how many hours the accountancy firm Dixon Wilson must have spent looking through the blog of *La Petite Anglaise* before they discovered the two afternoons when she played hooky. If companies choose repression they will be forced to establish their own departments of censorship and their own secret police.

Besides, corporate repression of this kind belongs to a world which is no more, where employees stood silently by the door, cap in hand, bowing and scraping. The world of work has changed, and since they are the ones who initiated the changes, employers should know this better than anyone. What can it possibly mean to 'bring a company into disrepute' in a world where half of the workforce routinely is fired every time a new CEO takes over? What does 'trust' mean in an office where computers and cameras monitor your every move? Why should you be loyal to a company which so obviously is not loyal to you?

In this new and far more insecure world, your only source of protection lies in your personal achievements and in the friendships you can strike up. Your blog helps promote both.

The blog showcases your talents and it connects you to a larger world. In the new labour market success comes to those who stand out, while the people who get screwed are the ones who keep their heads down and hope for the best. It actually might be safer to blog.

Not surprisingly, many of the fired bloggers have done very well for themselves. Heather Armstrong, the original doocee, is now blogging full-time and supporting a husband, a dog and a daughter through ads on her site. Ian Lind continues to work as an investigative reporter, but he is now employed by his own web page. Ellen Simonetti and the *Opinionista* both have book deals. *La Petite Anglaise* has a book deal too in addition to her court victory and a year's back wages. Joe Gordon has a great new job where he is blogging on the company's time. Kelly Kreth is still in the real estate business. As a result of a series of corporate takeovers, she is now the boss of the boss who once dooced her. Sweet revenge.

6

A Republic of Bloggers

Let's talk politics. Talking politics is easy, at least if you live in a democracy. People in a democracy may disagree about what you can say in a university or a workplace but they cannot disagree about the value of political discussions. As long as you talk politics you can say whatever you like. Our democracy wouldn't survive without vigorous debate, without dissent.

But if democracies are so full of vigorous debates why is it that voters often hold the most erroneous of beliefs? Critical scrutiny is supposed to flush out falsehoods and promote truths. But when the war in Iraq began, for example, 70 per cent of Americans believed that Saddam Hussein was behind the 9/11 attacks. And two years later, in February 2005, a third of Americans still believed that Iraq had had weapons of mass destruction at the time of the invasion. The rest of the world laughed at such ignorance. 'How can the Americans be so stupid?' Well, Americans aren't stupid, they're just badly informed. Ever since 9/11 American newspapers and TV stations have banged so loudly on their jingoistic drums that even when the truth occasionally was spoken it could not be heard.

Democracy requires free elections, but free elections are not enough to make a political system democratic. In addition, democracy requires an electorate which is enlightened enough to make well informed choices. On this measure, it is doubtful whether the US should be called a democracy. Clearly American voters are not sufficiently well informed to protect their own best interests. Or rather, democracy is a variable and not a constant. Perhaps the US is a 60 per cent democracy, 60 per cent critical scrutiny and 40 per cent ignorance.

While democracy gives one vote to every voter, mass media – at least in the US – is taken to be a market like any other. And just like in other markets, a few, very large, oligopolistic companies have emerged. They compete about viewers much in the way car companies compete about customers – by catering to the lowest common denominator in taste. Why are next to all cars silver-coloured? Why did next to all US news programmes in the run-up to the Iraq War regurgitate Bushisms? Because it makes financial sense, that's why. The truth matters less than the bottom line.

Control over mass media allows for a new form of authoritarian rule even in democratic societies. In addition to the US, Silvio Berlusconi's Italy provides an example. On the surface not a thing has changed. Universal elections are still being held, politics is still discussed, but in reality the old democratic order has been overturned. In Italy too media is an oligopoly, information is restricted and political options are constrained. People's world views are manipulated much as they were in the traditional dictatorships of yore. OK, the manipulations are not as sinister but the voters are manipulated just the same.

In the so called 'new' democracies such neo-authoritarianism blends seamlessly with authoritarianism of the traditional kind. In Russia or Thailand, the leaders can boast about their democratic credentials while closing down independent TV stations and newspapers. It is easy to imagine that the few remaining old-style dictatorships before long will go down this route. The day will surely come when even China has free and fair elections although the Communist Party retains full control over what's said in the media.

The good news is that the internet can help break up such media monopolies. The internet has the same universal reach as traditional mass media and it is far, far cheaper. Since entry costs are low, competition is fierce and since the bloggers are many, they are difficult to control. Even in China, a blogger with an account in the US and access to a public computer has a reasonable chance of disseminating unauthorized opinions. At least for a while.

In France, bloggers were prosecuted in November 2005 for coordinating riots in the Parisian suburbs, and a high school teacher – Étienne Chouard – is widely credited with swaying many French to vote against the political establishment and reject the European constitution in May 2005. In the UK, blogs have inspired political action too. Between 2002 and 2004 the *Bloggerheads* website conducted a series of stunts designed to investigate the power of blogs. One of the more successful campaigns included blog and SMS-coordinated protesters 'baring their bums at Bush' during the President's visit to Britain in November 2003.

Blogs can expose not only bums but also liars and hypocrites, and in the process they help improve our democracy. Blogs allow us to ask more questions and to give more answers. Blogs inspire and help coordinate political action. 'This is a great thing', politicians in democratic countries like to say. 'Western values regarding freedom of speech must be universally applied.' Especially, let's add, to the West itself.

Bloggers at the front line

Once the Iraq War got under way, the self-censorship practiced by US media was combined with restrictions imposed by the government. Journalists could report from the field, but only if they were 'embedded' with the troops. Being protected by the military provided journalists with unprecedented access but it also distorted their view of the conflict. Graphic images of wounded and dead American soldiers have been exceedingly rare, and photos of coffins returning home are censored. This is in sharp contrast with the Vietnam War where just such pictures helped spur anti-war demonstrations.

This presents a great opportunity for a blogger who really knows what's going on. For, let's say, an English-speaking Iraqi with an internet connection or a US soldier with a laptop in his Humvee. Bypassing the press briefings and the official rhetoric, blogs allow them to provide their own accounts of the war as they experience it. A click of the mouse gives you the story of the soldier shooting and another click gives you the story of the person being shot at.

The first blogs by American soldiers appeared already in the run-up to the war. 'Greyhawk' started his *Mudville Gazette* in the fall of 2002 in order to give soldiers a voice in which to speak directly to the public. Today, he links to over 400 military blogs, or milblogs, but the total number of blogging US soldiers may be closer to 1,000. They blog in order to stay in touch with family and friends back home, but also in order to interact with a larger audience. A blog's daily readership becomes an image of those 'ordinary Americans' who the soldiers were sent to war to fight for.

> I saw 2 guys creeping around this corner ... hiding behind a stack of truck tires. I saw another guy come out of that corner with an RPG [rocket-propelled grenade] in his hands. I freaked. I gathered my composure as fast as I could, put the cross hairs on them and engaged them. ... I didn't see anybody move from behind those tires after that.

Many soldiers use their blogs to make sense of gruesome experiences like this and to help explain themselves to themselves. Blogs also help restore a sense of normalcy to their lives. If nothing else, blogging gives them something to do while waiting for the next battle. One soldier, Jonathan Trouern-Trend, uses his *Birding Babylon* blog to record the birds he spots through his military binoculars. Others put up photo-blogs showing pictures of camels, dilapidated cities, young men horsing around.

The best of the writing – Colby Buzzell's *My War* blog is a great example – contains adrenaline-pumping accounts directly from the battlefield. There is the absurdity and confusion of war but also tales of camaraderie and unselfish actions. Blogging soldiers are no doves – and they don't like 'hippies' – but they are equally disdainful of armchair generals and politicians who haven't themselves seen combat. Overall they seem to care little about the reasons for going to war and very much about staying alive.

Click, click and we get to *Baghdad Burning*, *Iraqi Letter to America*, *Iraqi Roulette* and *The Daily Absurdity Report*. There are, according to *Iraq Blog Count*, some 241 English language blogs maintained by Iraqis. Since they are English-speaking and have internet connections, the bloggers are almost certainly well-educated and quite well off. The kind of people, in other words, who the Americans thought they could rely on to support the occupation. Sure enough, the bloggers were jubilant when they fired up their computers back in 2003 and wrote their first entries. Jubilations have since ceased. The author of the *Treasure of Baghdad* blog grieves for his mother, killed in a mortar attack. 'Sunshine' the 14-year old author of the *Days of My Life* blog reports:

> I was working on the computer and heavy shooting started, mortars fell on the neighborhood, this lasted for an hour, 3 mortars fell in the street, 2 in the street behind our house, and one in front of it.
>
> The poor widow who used to clean my class was killed, I feel really sorry for her children, they lost their parents, the cleaner before her was also killed.

Strikingly, ordinary Iraqis seem to write for very much the same reasons as do American soldiers – to let people know what they are going through, to deal with their fear and to explain themselves to themselves.

Many of the soldiers' immediate commanders seem to be reasonably supportive of the blogging habits of their men. On condition, of course, that they don't divulge sensitive information. Or perhaps, the Pentagon simply failed to understand the power of the medium they were dealing with. Said a spokesperson in 2004, 'We treat them the same way we would if they were writing a letter or speaking to a reporter: It's just information.'

But the Pentagon wizened up. In October 2006, the restrictions tightened and all milblogs are now subject to pre-publication censorship. Ten members of the Virginia National Guard are reportedly going through hundreds of thousands of web pages every month looking for security breaches. Since the bloggers are the ones whose lives are in danger – and since they generally are pro-Bush and pro-war – these restrictions make little sense to them. 'It seems we are denied the very liberties we are fighting for.'

The truth is of course that politicians and military commanders are equally afraid of the voices of the soldiers and of Iraqi civilians. Both speak with the authority of people who have stared death in the face. And they are, as they constantly repeat, sick of the misrepresentations and the ra-ra rhetoric. 'You don't know shit!'

There is no doubt that blogs – including staunchly pro-war blogs – undermine the war effort. Once you start reading the accounts given by Iraqi civilians it becomes impossible to treat their deaths as so much 'collateral damage'. And once you start reading the accounts of the soldiers, it becomes impossible to regard war as a heroic enterprise.

Broadcast yourself

If you don't trust mainstream media to broadcast the truth, you can broadcast it yourself on the *YouTube* website. On *YouTube* you can upload, view and share the videos of your choice – home-made, public domain or otherwise acquired. Say, for example, that you happen to record the hanging of an Iraqi dictator on your cell phone. Say further that regular TV stations refuse to show the material. What do you do? Of course, you post the stuff on www.youtube.com.

Launched in May 2005, *YouTube* quickly grew to become one of the most popular websites. Its users view some 100 million clips per day and 65,000 new clips are added daily. *YouTube* is also the site preferred by video bloggers – especially by celebrity wannabes displaying cleavage and pouty mouths. It's better than putting the videotaped diaries on your own site. Video files are unwieldy and and if you let *YouTube* host them you can save file space. And above all – on *YouTube* everyone in the whole world can see you.

Not everything goes, however. According to the official guide-lines, you can't post pornography or videos showing dangerous or illegal acts, gratuitous violence, hate speech, harassment or predatory behaviour. The videos aren't screened but all users can report offensive material and the clips are then removed. *YouTube* is often accused of unjustified and erratic censorship. In February 2007, for example, a video with readings from the Koran was taken down and the account of the uploader suspended. And the guy didn't even make any personal comments, he just read from the original text.

YouTube is great for whistle-blowers. In August 2006, Michael De Kort, a former engineer with Lockheed Martin, the large US defence contractor, used *YouTube* to report some pretty damaging facts about the way a contract with the Coast Guard had been handled. A range of old patrol boats was to be 'refurbished for the post-9/11 world', but the communications systems were easy to eavesdrop on and the boats weren't able to deal with extreme weather. De Kort had discussed these problems at various levels within Lockheed Martin, and with the Department of Homeland Security, but no one had listened to him. *YouTube* viewers however did, and before long not only the video but the topic itself was discussed all over mainstream media. 'Anybody with a webcam and something to say, regardless of whether it's true or not, can say it on *YouTube*', complained a Lockheed spokeswoman.

Visually though whistle-blower videos are pretty poor. Usually it's just a guy talking straight into a camera. Videos exposing police brutality, however, provide far more action. In November 2006, a clip showing the arrest of William Cardenas, a 24-year old alleged gang member in Los Angeles, was posted on *YouTube*. It was graphic evidence indeed. Two officers can be seen holding him down on a Hollywood street. One punches him several times in the face before they are able to handcuff him. The tape clocked up 155,000 views in the first three weeks and the conduct of the officers was subject to investigations both by the LAPD and the FBI.

The authorities in many countries worry about this uncontrollable spread of information. In March 2007, a court in Turkey ordered the largest internet service provider, Turk Telecom, to block access to *YouTube* after a Greek blogger had said nasty things about Mustafa Kemal Atatürk, the country's founder. Apparently, Atatürk was a homosexual and an alcoholic. In Turkey, a law against 'the belittling of Turkishness' is regularly used to muzzle such critics. *YouTube* access was restored two days later once the video was taken down.

There are several other cases:

- In Brazil, *YouTube* access was blocked in January 2007 after videos of the model and local MTV host, Daniela Cicarelli, were discovered. The celebrity complained that the flicks, showing her and her boyfriend making love on a Spanish beach, were illegally obtained.
- In the Australian state of Victoria, *YouTube* was banned in schools when videos showing 'degrading attacks' on a 17-year old Melbourne schoolgirl were posted by male students.
- Brigham Young University, the Mormon outfit in Utah, is also blocking *YouTube*. There is too much violence and smut on the website, a spokesperson for the university explained, and students spend too much time watching it.

In Britain too the government is in principle in favour of censorship of *YouTube*. Again, the reason is the alleged broadcasting of indiscriminate violence. According to Jack Straw, the former Home Secretary and current Lord Chancellor and Justice Secretary, 'There is a very serious issue how such videos should better be controlled.'

Too much freedom?

But perhaps the Turkish authorities and Jack Straw have a point? Perhaps, sometimes, too much information can be a bad thing? After all, democracy becomes very chaotic if everyone is talking at the same time, or if people say too many irresponsible and bigoted things. Often enough the right to free speech is just a pretext for deliberately misinforming the public.

In the past, during the days of editorial control, these problems were dealt with through voluntary codes and self-regulation. It was all very gentleman-like. You just weren't supposed to say certain things in a newspaper or on the air. And the editors made sure you didn't. Blogs and assorted outspoken websites have shattered this consensus. There is no time for niceties – bring on the bigotry!

Consider the following, pretty nauseating, samples:

- *Knights of the KKK* – 'Between 1906 and 1991 the Ku Klux Klan lynched around 20 Negroes. In contrast, in 1991 alone 1,300 Negroes killed each other in gang warfare.'
- *Stormfront* – 'White pride, worldwide.'
- *Killbattyman* – Jamaican blog advocating the execution of gays.
- *The First Amendment Exercise Machine* – 'Race mixing is genocide.'
- *The Church of Euthanasia* – 'The four pillars: suicide, abortion, cannibalism, sodomy.'

- *IslamaNazi.com* – 'How about rooting for America for a change you liberal scumbag?'
- *Zundelsite* – 'Did 6 million really die?'

Or take the case of blogs whose sole purpose is to slag off various politicians. Sites like *Anne Milton, Guildford MP (and Dipstick)*; *AnyOneButKen*; *Blairwatch*; *FibDems*; *Impeach Bush Coalition*; *MakeSurreyLibDemFree*; *www.Anti-Bush.com* and many others.

Somewhere between information and misinformation we have conspiracy theories. Cranks peddling various amazing explanations have of course always existed but the web has greatly increased the size of their audience.

- *Is Bush Wired.com* – 'Is he prompted through an ear piece?'
- *Joe Vialls, Private Investigator* – 'Prince Charles implicated in the murder of Princess Diana.'
- *Scholars for 9/11 Truth* – 'The impact of the planes cannot have caused enough damage to bring the buildings down, since the buildings were designed to withstand them.'
- *The Apollo Hoax* – 'The faked Apollo landings: evidence of National Aeronautics and Space Administration, NASA, airbrushing out moon anomalies.'
- The discussion forum at *AboveTopSecret.com* – 'Are Indian mangoes an instrument of mind-control?' 'Is Saddam Hussein still alive?' 'Does Google collect our deoxyribonucleic acid, DNA?' And the ultimate paranoia: 'Are discussion boards on conspiracy theory websites controlled by the Jews?'

It just could be true, you know? Can you prove that it isn't true? Prove that it isn't true and I'll believe you!

In Germany, where it is a crime to deny that the holocaust happened and offenders can be put in prison for up to five years, the authorities have forced internet service providers to close down Nazi websites. Germany has also tried to restrict access to foreign websites with objectionable content. The results are mixed. Access to the revisionist *Zundelsite* was temporarily blocked, but when mirror sites quickly sprang up in the US – maintained by neo-Nazis or by freedom of speech advocates – the German authorities had to admit defeat. Still Google's search results are filtered in Germany, making it far less likely that innocent web-surfers come into contact with offensive material. In fact, Google filters searches in France too.

Brits have also discussed restrictions. New Labour under Tony Blair was famously trying to micro-manage the flow of information. When media misbehaved – such as the BBC during the run-up to the Iraq War – they were quickly bullied into submission. Not surprisingly, the Blair government disliked blogs. In November 2006, Matthew Taylor, Blair's Chief Adviser on political strategy, complained publicly about the 'shrill discourse of demands' created by personal web pages. People at large, he said, are encouraged to regard all politicians as corrupt and mendacious. It is 'a conspiracy to maintain the population in a perpetual state of self-righteous rage'. Part of the problem was what Taylor referred to as the 'net-head culture' of the internet, 'rooted in libertarianism and anti-establishment attitudes'. The net should not be used to abuse politicians, he warned, 'or make incommensurate demands on them'.

For bloggers who had wondered what to write about that day, Taylor's comments came as a blessing. Clearly this was a first taste of some new piece of legislation that Blair was cooking up in his Number 10 kitchen. It didn't smell good! Making the most of their freedom while it lasted, the blogosphere consulted their thesauri for more anti-Blairite invectives.

Let's be very crude about this. Let's count the dead bodies. How many people have died as a result of the irresponsible use of blogs and how many have died as a result of oligopolistic, or government control over media? Of course there are more racist slurs and unconfirmed rumours in blogs, and one could possibly imagine that there are blog entries that inspire their readers to commit crimes. Let's be generous and say that 100 people are killed worldwide every year as a result of blog-inspired actions.

Compare this with the thousands upon thousands of people killed as a result of government actions which aren't properly discussed in the media. The American war in Iraq is a good case in point. The medical journal, *The Lancet*, famously put this figure at 600,000 dead Iraqis. Surely, some of them could have been saved if US newspapers and TV stations had been less jingoistic and better at critically discussing Bush's reasons for going to war.

It's not very nice to defend holocaust deniers, cannibals and other monsters. If given half a chance most of us would much rather defend causes that give us warm and fuzzy feelings. But these are not cases that involve the freedom of speech. As long as we all agree with one another, freedom of speech is not at stake. The test of our commitment to free speech is rather whether we extend the right also to the people we dislike the most.

In the end only private individuals can prevent the public mistakes committed by the state. This is why individuals must have the right to speak freely and why freedom of speech must be given unique protection. It is only private irresponsibility which can check public irresponsibility. Private irresponsibility should be encouraged to the extent that it helps prevent the far greater irresponsibility of governments. If a few racist slurs and unconfirmed rumours is the price we have to pay to prevent future disastrous wars, what we need is more racism and more unconfirmed rumours.

The new populism

But blogging is not only a threat to the politicians. It's also a new opportunity for them. Politicians too, after all, can take up the habit. Much like the CEOs of companies they can use blogs to re-brand their shop-worn wares. By speaking directly and personally, they can connect with new demographics, launch new ideas and get instantaneous feedback on them. They can also raise money and mobilize people to act in their support. And not least, blogs allow politicians to bypass the editors. Politicians too, after all, often complain about being 'misquoted' and 'misrepresented' by traditional media.

Not surprisingly, lots of politicians have become bloggers in recent years: David Milliband, David Cameron and Boris Johson in the UK; John Edwards, Ralph Nader, Howard Dean and Jerry Brown in the US; ex-Prime Minister Paul Martin in Canada; EU's Vice President Margot Wallström; French presidential-hopeful Ségolène Royal and Hungary's Prime Minister Ferenc Gyurcsany. Germany's Chancellor Angela Merkel is vlogging no less, podcasting on *YouTube*. There is also an impressive list of authoritarian and post-authoritarian rulers who blog: Muammar al-Gaddafi of Libya, Iran's Mahmoud Ahmadinejad, Juwono Sudarsono, the Indonesian Minister of Defence, Prince Norodom Sihanouk of Cambodia.

It's surely wonderful that our betters deign to talk to us in this fashion. It's like they actually cared. Perhaps, after all, they aren't just ruling us but also trying to engage us in some kind of conversation? If you think Iran's nuclear programme poses a threat to the stability of the Middle East, leave a message on Ahmadinejad's blog. If you don't like the Tory's EU policy, let David Cameron know. In fact, since it's so easy to communicate in this way, we suddenly become suspicious of politicians who don't do it. Why isn't Gordon Brown blogging, or George Bush, or Elizabeth II? It's like they don't give a damn.

Or are the politicians just fooling us? After all, the intentions – even the identity – of a blogging politician are just as easy to doubt as the intentions and identities of other bloggers. Why is it, for example, that leading US politicians only blog during election campaigns? Do any of them ever read the comments we leave? And why do many of the blog entries sound so wooden? Of course, they were written by some hack at party headquarters!

The challenge, in other words, is just the same as that faced by company CEOs. Blogs are not press releases. Somehow or another you have to make the words believable. If all they do is to repeat the same old message, they lose their authority together with their audience. Blogs are a self-revelatory, confessional and ass-kicking medium, but self-revelations, confessions and ass-kicking is exactly what get politicians into trouble. And they know it. Besides, if it doesn't come naturally to you, you should probably not bother. Stuffy politicians shouldn't wear baseball caps pointing backwards when meeting members of ethnic minorities and they shouldn't jive in their blogs. If they do, they have misunderstood the rules of engagement with the general public.

In the end it's only the politicians with an 'inner blogger' who successfully can pull it off. Politicians, that is, with a need to express themselves regardless of the electoral benefits and the impact on their careers. Consider the following three examples:

- The Swedish politician, Carl Bildt, started a blog in 2005 as a means of commenting on the day's events in politics and in his personal life. When he became the Foreign Minister a year later he took a couple of month's break before returning to his blog. A decision prompted not least – as he noted – by the fact that the foreign ministry's official web pages were so dreadfully dull.
- Garth Turner, an MP for the Conservative Party in Canada, uses his *Garth Turner Unedited* as a means of reporting from parliament on behalf of his constituents. As a former newspaper journalist, blogging comes naturally to him. A topic which particularly excited him in 2006 was the decision of a former Liberal Party minister to defect to the Conservative Party. Turner's conclusions on the subject were as blunt as they were unauthorized.
- Bob Piper is a Labour Councillor from Sandwell in the West Midlands who peppers his *Bob Piper Blog* with assorted Bob Dylan quotes and down-at-the pub banter. Unusually in Blair's New Labour, Piper is not taking orders from central party headquarters. He is anti-war,

pro-union, and he has the unusual habit of calling lying hypocrites 'lying hypocrites'. Great stuff.

Their inner blogger is what got all three into trouble. In October 2006, Garth Turner was expelled from his party for 'compromising caucus confidentiality'. Above all, it seems, for the blog-entries about the Liberal ex-minister. Meanwhile, Bob Piper was raked over the coals for posting a picture showing David Cameron, the Tory leader, as a black-faced minstrel. Was Piper a racist? No, but he may have been a fool. Carl Bildt too was accused of being reckless. His blog became a topic of national controversy in Sweden in February 2007. We can't have a frank and self-revelatory foreign minister, some concluded. Diplomats, after all, aren't supposed to actually say anything when they speak.

It is surely sad that politicians get into trouble for using their own voices online. We don't want to be ruled by *apparatchiki* who stick to the party line. Inner bloggers too should be able to run for public office. But we must at the same time be careful not to be seduced by this public intimacy. As voters, we need to hold politicians accountable. We need to judge their policies in a dispassionate manner. This becomes even more difficult when we come to think of them as people we are familiar with. In the blogs the politicians are in complete control of messages which most of us have no way of checking. Blogs in the end become just another way of pulling the wool over our eyes. As always, *caveat internet-surfor*!

A public sphere which is increasingly intimate in nature is a public sphere which is evermore privatized. And if the public sphere is privatized we no longer properly speaking live in a republic. There is no 'thing' – *res* – which is 'common' – *publica*. Instead we share only each other's intimacies. Intimacies can't be political and they can't be contested. In a privatized public sphere we feel a lot but we don't think very much and we don't argue over matters of principle.

This is exactly why blogs are appealing to many populist politicians in dictatorships or new – or shall we say 'post-neo' – democracies. Populist politicians want to seduce rather than convince, and they always prefer to bypass the awkward questions asked by reporters and talk directly to the people. The internet is the newest means of fulfilling this populist dream.

From this perspective we should perhaps be grateful that our leaders generally are such technological illiterates. Bill Clinton sent only two emails while in office and there is something almost endearing about Bush's references to 'the internets' and to that time he was searching 'the Google'. An affable, blogging, warmonger of a president is just what we don't need.

A republic of bloggers?

Blogs are great for breaking up media monopolies and for disseminating information. We get the latest word, unfiltered, straight from the place where things happen and from the people involved. Blogs are great also for starting and sustaining debates. Suddenly there is a chorus of new voices, far more interesting and better articulated than we'd ever imagine. This is surely great for democracy. A society won't remain a democracy for long unless voters are well informed and discussions are vigorous.

Of course some of the voices – occasionally the loudest ones – are bigoted and malicious. Sometimes the information conveyed is misinformation. Not surprisingly, people with repressive tendencies will try to pull the plug on the whole business. Consider the following arguments in favour of blog censorship:

- Blogs legitimate dangerous ideas which previously were given no legitimation. Young and gullible people are particularly likely to be influenced.
- The ideas are not only dangerous but also contagious. They quickly pass from one blog to the other, infecting them all.
- Blogs provide organizational resources to groups advocating reprehensible programmes. Blogs help

coordinate the activities of groups that operate with non-democratic methods.

- Public deliberation is undermined. Arguments become exaggerated and shrill and no one listens to anyone else or cares to try to reach a common consensus.

There is a patriarchal and condescending tone to these arguments. They presuppose that people can't make a distinction between respectable and non-respectable sources. And that most people are latent bigots and that elites have an obligation to stop them from following their basest instincts.

Whatever merits these arguments may have had in the old public sphere, they are quite irrelevant in the public sphere created by the internet. Today, there is no longer one discussion in which everyone participates. There are instead tens of thousands of discussions taking place simultaneously all over the web. There isn't one big room, as it were, but tens of thousands of small ones. On the internet public expressions are plentiful, cheap, and they have no particular authority and bestow no legitimacy. They don't even reach very far. In the end it's just some guy sounding off to a few friends.

People are also expressing themselves quite differently. They are not spokespersons making official statements but ordinary people speaking informally, and often rather incoherently. Private individuals have taken over and the public sphere has become privatized.

Not surprisingly, the rules that govern public speech will be those that always have governed private speech. In private, people have always said all kinds of racists and bigoted things. It's not nice to be sure, but we've learned to put up with it. In exactly the same way we are today going to have to learn to live with bigotry on the web. Let the nutters eat their own nuts. And, as we argued, this is the lesser of two evils. The greater evil are restrictions on information enforced by state monopolies or by privately-run, ra-ra, oligopolies.

The real problem with political blogs is rather that they make us focus far too much on talk and not nearly enough on action. It is easy to do politics online but for that very reason it is also often futile. Let's face it, sounding off on one topic after another in your blog isn't going to change anything. If you want to have an impact what you need is real power. You need organizational resources, money and boots on the ground. The internet can help in these respects too – as Howard Dean's web-savvy presidential bid proved in 2004. But it's always going to be difficult to organize and mobilize people who are connected to each other mainly through the internet.

A hope is sometimes expressed that 'cyber-communities' can come to replace ordinary political communities. And there are certainly examples of such communities being created – not least around blogs. Yet we should not forget how poor and superficial relations between people are online. Sitting alone in front of our computers we are next to completely anonymous to one another. On a website we come and go but we rarely make long and lasting commitments to each other. A cyber-community is to a real community like casual sex is to marriage.

7

Secrets of the Heart

Most people go to considerable lengths to protect their privacy. They don't want others to pry into their secrets. Our heart is our castle and trespassers are shot on sight. Yet some other people, strangely, seem to have no respect for the sanctity of their own private realms. Happily inviting trespassers to have a look around, they share the most intimate details of their lives. How many moles they have on their bottoms and what exactly happened on the night their fathers died.

This contrast – between the anally retentive and the anally expulsive – has always existed but it has been augmented by blogs. Today it's so much easier to let it all hang out in public. But why would you expose your private life to millions of readers? And why publicize facts to strangers which you wouldn't even tell your bestest friend?

A common explanation invokes a commitment to truth. Some people just don't like hypocrisy. They don't like lies, they tell us, they have nothing to hide and nothing to be ashamed of. To live truthfully is to live in such a way that one always is prepared to give an account of one's life. A blog can be such an account. It's known as 'blogging naked', blogging with the aim of revealing it all.

But such explanations are surely not sufficient. Much alleged truth-telling is really nothing but the spinning of yet another yarn. We kiss and tell but the public persona we create in the process is actually nothing like ourselves. Peeling off one layer of skin reveals nothing but another layer. This is not truth-telling as much as narrative self-construction and identity play. The blogging, unblogging and reblogging of ourselves online.

Significantly, alleged truth-telling and narrative play seems to be particularly important for people who for one reason or another are insecure about who they are. People in transit from childhood to adulthood, for example, or from middle-age to old age. Truth-telling is often an imperative for people who struggle with sexual identities, childhood traumas, with experiences of war or miscarriages of justice. They just can't stand secrecy. And they can't accept the identities foisted on them by mainstream society.

For people like this, blogs provide a way of breaking through the walls of silence. For years and years homosexuality or child abuse were not issues of public concern. But once such issues were picked up by mainstream media, their treatment was determined by editorial filters. 'Not abused wives again', many an editor was heard exclaiming, 'we did that last week!' Happily those days are gone. Today, no editors can stop us. If we want to talk about our bulimia, our fear of death, or our sexual impotence in public, we'll just do it.

The experience of speaking out is itself liberating as well as empowering. Around many a self-revelatory blog, communities of people with similar experiences are created. People read, leave comments, participate in discussions. 'You know', a generic blog comment reads, 'I thought I was alone in feeling like this.' 'Exactly the same thing happened to me!' 'I suspect my husband is gay/ seeing someone else/ is on the verge of a mental breakdown.'

Still there are limits to self-expression even here. There are things we can't and shouldn't say. This is not an issue of what you legally are allowed to say or what you might get yourself fired for. Rather it's a matter of what it's prudent to reveal about oneself. Where are – to use an old-fashioned expression – the limits of decency and decorum?

The whole hog blog

Meet Justin Hall. Justin began his online journal in 1994, as a 19-year old freshman at Swarthmore College. That is to say, he had an online presence way before all others. In a sense it was Justin Hall who invented blogging. Not as a technology to be sure, but as a public expression of a person's life. Like other teenagers he was desperate to communicate with people around him, yet no one cared to listen.

> I found a letter that my father wrote after the birth of my brother where he extolled the virtues of raising children with nannies – 'You only have to see the child for an hour a day, at feeding time.'

His blog, Justin was determined, was going to be his means of reaching out. He was going to tell it all. Every secret, every triumph, every embarrassment. The whole hog. To put himself, his family and friends online – and on the line.

> My father was a wry, humanistic, sensitive man and an intolerant, spiteful, bastard. … Conservative as hell, he wrote curmudgeonly letters … had a decent gun collection. … An alcoholic for many years before he met my mother. … There was little she could do to stave his descent into depression …

When Justin was eight his father killed himself, and naturally we get a scan of the suicide note. 'I can't really remember his voice but I still dream about him.'

Why is Justin writing all this? In a video he posted on *YouTube* when he retired from blogging 11 years later, he explains, 'The web makes me not alone. And I feed it my intimacies and the web is my constant connection to something larger than myself.' It's like communicating with God or like a simultaneous orgasm. 'When someone comes you know they are there for just a moment. And you feel like maybe what you're feeling someone else feels. That's what I wanted online.'

In these respects a blog resembles a confession. Institutionalized at the Fourth Lateran Council in 1215, the confession, to quote the *Catholic Encyclopedia*, 'is a judicial process in which the penitent is at once the accuser, the person accused, and the witness'. The sinner presents himself to God, identifies his crimes, is judged, sentenced and then forgiven. Compare a blog in which you unburden yourself before your readers, asking for their empathy and understanding. As a result, you no longer single-handedly have to carry the weight of your fears and your desires.

> I feel like a real veteran of the sexual revolution, engaging in free love cost me a few weeks of peeing pain. In a heated moment of passion at Swarthmore, I was with a woman, we were fairly intoxicated, screwing without protection. ... A few days later, I noticed a strange smell in the shower, when I was cleaning my penis.

And let's not forget, to reveal things is exciting. Secrets, if sufficiently juicy, shock and grab people's attention. Telling them, we steal the limelight and make jaws drop. Revealing secrets makes us feel important. In some cases it can become something akin to a Turrett's syndrome – just because we shouldn't tell, we'll go ahead and tell it. And once we've started, we can't stop.

> I often use computers to stimulate my jacking off since I'm so often sitting at my computer, and alone then, it's not unusual for a late night surfing session to become waylaid

by wet thoughts. I stopped collecting porno pictures when I was like fifteen, they do take up too much room on my hard drive.

Relationship resume, 1992–present. Experience with a number of women and one man learning about physical pleasure and emotional stimulation. Penetrative sex with a total of twenty-six people, ranging in age from sixteen to thirty-eight. Fifteen of these exchanges were one-evening insertions.

Justin Hall became an internet phenomenon. Thousands of curious daily readers followed his confessions. And even when the material was repulsive – and some of his revelations were – that only seemed to increase the attraction. Like car crashes, Saddam Hussein's hanging, or various online fetishes, web-surfers just couldn't make themselves look away.

Finally, in January 2005, after some 4,800 entries, Justin Hall suddenly stopped. Something was wrong with the whole online experiment. In the *YouTube* clip he explains why. Online relationships just weren't enough. The internet was 'all pulp and no fluid', just 'shreds of connection'. But when Justin found a new woman he was forced to choose. She didn't want to be exposed online and Justin realized he had to give up blogging. He traded his art for a better, more private life. But he was scared until the last moment and in the video he is in tears. Does it make sense to sacrifice a thousand virtual relationships for one big relationship offline? But what if that offline experiment doesn't work out?

After the *YouTube* video, his original blog went off the air. Today Justin Hall is still blogging, but now he does it like a proper adult – about computer games and the internet, society and cultural trends. There's no more juicy stuff. It's probably significant that he was 19 when he started blogging naked and that he stopped right after turning 30. He too grew up in the end. Good for him perhaps, but too bad for his readers.

Teenage blogs

Justin Hall's early blogging experiment is today repeated in a slightly more timid form in hundreds of thousands of teenage blogs. The typical blogger, we said, is not a political dissident, a maverick professor or a cyber-geek. She is a teenage girl spilling her heart out online. To other bloggers – serious and grown-up bloggers – these blogs are an embarrassment. The topics are trivial, the writing is poor, the emotions may be deeply felt but they are terribly badly expressed. The blogs aren't even updated regularly. 'Most of it is pure crap', say the bloggers on the A-list to their hundreds of thousands of readers, 'these are the people who give blogging a bad name'.

But wait a minute. Doesn't anyone remember what it was like to be a teenager? Teenagers are no longer children but they are not yet grown-ups. They have schools to go to, social relations to sort out, problems understanding the expectations of parents and other authority figures. They are often angry, confused about sex, and they engage in all kinds of risk-taking behaviour. So what if your blog is crap and you have no readers? If blogging is what you have to do, you have to do it. Who else but your imaginary readers are going to listen to you?

Just as in the case of university students, blogs are often combined with more social formats. *MySpace*, with over 100 million registered users, is the most celebrated example. Created in 2003, and now owned by Rupert Murdoch's News Corporation, *Myspace* much like *Facebook*, is a website where you leave personal data about yourself. You list your interests, favourite movies and bands, and whatever else that describes you, including a 'person I'd like to meet' section. Photos, music and videos can be added too together with notes and traditional blog entries.

MySpace is highly socially competitive. It's a place to brag and show off. Guys pose with gun collections and girls in their most alluring outfits. Imagine if you could reach those 100 million people, how famous you'd be! Or as the *Urban Dictionary* explains, 'it becomes a competition of seeing who has the most friends, so you add everyone you've made eye contact with in the past 6 years'. It's a place where 'emo chicks tend to whore themselves out and show off their highly-contrasted badly-photographed selves – said chicks usually sporting a pout and cleavage'. Checking out chicks and guys and leaving messages quickly becomes addictive.

> However, after about a month or so, you finally realize that even though you had thousands of friends added, you're still a loser. … You eventually delete your account because you decide you want to graduate high school with some dignity.

It is easy to imagine what parents and teachers think of all this. Neither bloggers nor *MySpace* users, they quickly declare themselves 'concerned'. Premonitions of 'Jessica, 14, loves music and horses' who turns out to be 'Jerry, 41, with a history of stalking playgrounds', flash before their eyes. And there are reasons for such fears. Some pedophiles do indeed maintain honey-pot blogs designed to attract unsuspecting children, and *MySpace*, with its enormous catalogue of personal information, is a predator's dream. According to one study, one in seven children between the ages of ten and seventeen have been solicited for sex online.

In January 2007, four American families sued *MySpace* after their daughters had been abused by men who contacted them via the website. MySpace defended itself by saying that parents should monitor internet use by children more closely, and promised that they shortly will be installing new security software.

Cyber-bullying is another concern, albeit less obviously grievous. A cyber-bully may be a classmate who leaves threatening messages on someone's blog or on social networking sites. Or perhaps someone who sends demeaning text messages or emails with nasty photo-shopped images. To a child a cyber-bully can be just as tormenting as his schoolyard equivalent.

If nothing else, the concerned adults go on, compromising material could end up in the hands of prospective employers, prospective schools, and maybe even the police. God knows how many years into the future the material will be available online and who eventually will read it. If *MySpace* is a party, it's a party which grown-ups can observe through a one-way mirror. Admitting to recreational drug use is surely daft, and so is admitting to cheating in exams or posing with guns or too much cleavage.

Well-intentioned as such admonitions certainly are, they underestimate the fundamental need of teenagers to posture and to socialize. There is nothing frivolous or optional about these needs. Teenagers must express themselves just as much as children must play and grown-ups must work. You deny this need only to their detriment. Grown-ups whose identities have been thoroughly entrenched for decades will always have problems understanding this process of identity-creation.

And often enough what grown-ups really are concerned about is bourgeois respectability. All families have their secrets and parents just don't want their children to reveal them online. The prospective readers they worry about are not employers or schools, or even Jerry 41, but rather fellow members of their church or golf club or colleagues at work. 'How dare you? Blogging about us after all we've done for you!'

Teenage bloggers should be informed about the risks associated with blogged revelations. They need to understand the difference between the online and the offline world. But today's teenagers are, if anything, more likely than their parents to make this distinction. They know about identity-play since they engage in so much of it. At any rate, stopping them from blogging is foolish and against their best interests. As for bourgeois respectability, tough luck!

Love & hate online

Take the hardy perennial of a boy who loves a girl, who, for her part, insists that they are better off remaining 'just friends'. In the olden days you would compose a poem exposing the shrew, but today you talk about her in your blog. Here, revenge is sweeter than ever. Thanks to the internet the whole world will know what she is like and what injustices you suffered. It doesn't even have to be true. You can tell all her future prospective boyfriends about her ineptitude in bed and her bad case of STD. As your blog scales the heights of the Google rankings, you will slowly get your revenge.

In September 2006, Kyle, a 19-year old American, met the girl of his dreams. As an inveterate blogger, he naturally told the story online. At first he is only referring to her as 'M', – 'so she can retain her privacy' – but before long she turns into 'Miranda', a girl 'very intelligent, very cute and very much in touch with the world'. Not one to hold back, Kyle soon declares his undying love. Miranda, however, is not so sure. She 'needs space', she says, even before their relationship is off the ground. One day, after telling him she has to go home, Kyle spots her walking into a restaurant – with his room-mate of all people. At this point the blog descends into a mixture of abuse and self-pity. No one has ever loved as strongly as Kyle and no one has ever been more cruelly deceived. She is a 'selfish bitch' and his room-mate is a 'douche bag'.

Why is Kyle blogging about this? Because he is 19 years old and he needs to talk to someone. The blog is his therapy. It helps him, he says, 'to vent my anger and manage my stress'. Considering what he says about his family, and about his loneliness, the blog may be a more attentive audience than many people in the offline world. What complicates matters is that Kyle is using his real name, the real name of his school, of the girl and the room-mate. Naturally, this is distressing to the people concerned. Miranda leaves a comment under one of the posts telling him he is a self-destructive fool and that she is not worth getting mad at. There are heated exchanges with the room-mate and his friends.

At this point Kyle's college intervened. As a student at the same school, Miranda had complained to the teachers about the abusive entries and the teachers, not unreasonably, felt compelled to act. Soon afterwards Kyle was expelled. Yet he remains unrepentant. The fact that people can Google her name in the future is part of his revenge. Just google and Miranda's cruelty will be evident for all the world to see.

Of course Kyle acted irresponsibly. He shouldn't have accused Miranda of various imaginary crimes and he shouldn't have called her names. It's just not nice. On the other hand, it's not clear whether Kyle deserved to be punished. To the people directly involved the blog entries were certainly upsetting, but for anyone outside that small circle it's just the regular kind of stuff of which teenage romance is made. We go 'aaaaaaaahhhhh ... isn't that sweet!' even at his admissions of disappointment and rage. The feelings are strong but also very common and actually not all that interesting. And nothing of what Kyle says reflects badly on Miranda. Google or no Google, she has nothing to fear.

Much the same goes for Justin Hall's revelations. Although he is far, far more private than Kyle – in fact it's impossible to conceive of more intimate revelations – the result is not actually embarrassing neither to him nor to us. Since he is such a great writer, what he describes are not his private experiences but instead our common ones. We are not gawking at a freak but seeing ourselves more clearly.

Women of a certain age

The teenage years are a notorious time of identity crisis, but identity crises return whenever we are forced to move from one stage in our life cycle to another. Take the example of women of a certain age – past child-bearing, let's say, but before senior citizenship. Consider a professional woman, financially secure, divorced since a few years back. What's her identity? She's been a mother and a wife, a whore and a madonna, and the question is what she's going to be and do next. There are few social pointers for her to go by since independent women of this kind hardly existed in the past. She has to figure herself out. Just like teenagers she has to make up some self for herself.

Not surprisingly, woman-of-a-certain-age blogs – WoaCA blogs – have proliferated in recent years. Many WoaCA seize on political or cultural issues – perhaps religion or feminism – and the blog is ostensibly woven around that theme. The writing is more balanced and the writer doesn't seem as insecure, yet the blogs fulfil many of the same functions as teenage blogs. Even in a blog which seems to be about shopping, church-going or gardening we find unexpected confessions and pleas for existential confirmation.

BlogHer is a community portal of some 6,500 plus blogs written by women. You register and submit the address of your blog and you are added to the site's blogroll. A team of editors then scan the participating blogs and highlight interesting recent entries on the front page of the *BlogHer* website. 'It's about providing a global stage for women's personal printing presses', says *BlogHer*'s founder Lisa Stone.

Just as in the case of teenagers there is a lot of posturing going on. But it doesn't concern drug-taking and sex as much as the sweaters the ladies are knitting and the cakes they bake. Truth be told, much of the writing is profoundly tedious. There are, for example, endless photos of cats, discussions of what cats eat, how they sleep, and what could have happened to Snowy since she doesn't look quite well this morning. These are not, on the whole, blogs which the A-list of bloggers regard very highly. But so what? They are not written for a mass audience but instead primarily for the writer herself. Their tedium speaks of their profound personal relevance.

As respectable members of society, WoaCA authors are often concerned about what they can and cannot say online. 'How comfortable are you blogging naked?' asks a *BlogHer* editorial. 'Are you ready to reveal it all?' Everyone commenting remembers how they started out trying to be frank and forthcoming but quickly discovered that they couldn't do it. There are limits to the language you can use and the topics you can discuss. On the whole, the ladies don't say 'fuck' or admit to drug-taking. 'There are many things

I won't write about in my blog', says one of them, 'because my friends are reading, the members of my church and my husband's colleagues'. Ex-husbands are a particular obstacle to freedom of speech. 'Since my ex discovered my blog, I can no longer discuss him or he pitches a hissy', says one. 'I used to write about it all', says another, 'but I've changed'.

> my blog was the center of a custody trial and my rants were used to attack my character, especially things I said about my ex, and since I did not know he was reading, he would 'bait' me, and then wait to read what I wrote about what he did, and his wife would save the posts to use against me later.

Questions of freedom of speech have a particular relevance to the subversive cabal which is the world of online embroidery enthusiasts. A secret world rarely penetrated by outsiders, embroidery fans – predominantly women of a certain age – have recently taken up blogging en masse. On the web they share designs and photos of innovative stitches and tales of their embroidered successes. Some run their blogs like small businesses, selling CDs with patterns which visitors can buy. Embroidery enthusiasts are active posters, active commenters on each other's blogs, creating a befittingly pleasant pattern of a closely knit community.

This was when the Embroidery Software Protection Coalition struck. This association of large sewing companies had discovered that their copyrighted designs were floating around the web, exchanged for free or sold as the embroiders' own. They responded by sending out generalized 'cease and desist' letters to as many culprits as they could locate. Clearly, in many cases, they got the wrong people. Very upset about this treatment the embroiders began complaining to each other in online discussion groups. In some cases the words applied to the Embroidery Software Protection Coalition were those rarely seen on embroidered canvases.

The Coalition decided to go after them again, and subpoenaed Yahoo – which hosted the most vocal of these discussion groups – in order to get access to the offline identities of the most offensive posters. In its legal filing, it likened some of the online screeds to 'terrorist activities' and accused the ladies of posting slanderous statements 'that marched across the Internet bulletin boards and chat groups similar to Hitler's march across Europe'.

Not dying alone

Story-telling is probably never more important than when a life-threatening illness, or the very process of ageing, has taken us to the ultimate limits of our personality. Pausing on this final threshold before the blue screen of death, we need to take stock of our lives. If consolation ever is called for it is now.

In the olden days we would simply reminisce and look at old photos. Or if we were famous, we would write an autobiography or at least a column in a newspaper. There was an epidemic of such self-revelatory *feuilletons* in the papers in the 1990s where one famous person after another outed him or herself as having a life-threatening illness and then proceeded to write about the process of living and dying with it. Fascinating stuff for readers who got a rare glimpse of a celebrity at their most vulnerable. Comforting, no doubt, for the celebrities who got a chance to give voice to their fears.

But why should only famous people have a chance to unburden themselves? Why should ordinary people have to die alone?

In August 2002, Ivan Noble, a 35-year old technology journalist on BBC's website, started an online diary documenting his struggle with a brain tumour. It's all there, neatly documented: MRI scans and operations, post-op diagnoses, hopes that are kindled and then quashed. In January 2005, he wrote his last post:

> When I began writing about having a brain tumour, I did not really know why. That personal style of journalism was never something I was particularly attracted to or interested in reading myself. ...But when I was diagnosed back in

2002 I had a strong urge to fight back against what felt like the powerlessness of the situation. I know now that people have found the diary useful… The regular feedback from dozens and dozens of people every time I have written has been wonderful, especially in real times of crises.

As always when confronting the unfairness of death, we struggle in vain to justify it. Why him and not us? Many of his readers tried their best to cheer Ivan on and encouraged him to look on the bright side of life. Yet, somehow or another their attempts at encouragement weren't very reassuring. In the end Ivan's final logging off was accompanied by a chorus of trite, pseudo-religious platitudes. Blog or no blog, when we really are staring the inevitability of death in the face, meaning-making itself stops making sense.

Not all life-threatening illnesses actually kill us of course, and maybe blogs are more useful for people on remission. Take the case of breast cancer blogs, documented by portals such as *MyBreastCancerNetwork.com*. Here, women write revealingly about the experiences of being diagnosed and treated, what it's like to receive news of the illness, what it's like to go through chemotherapy and endless operations. Not all accounts are happy of course, but most blogs offer encouraging advice and upbeat, 'you-can-get-through-it' messages.

Jeannette, in her *Two Hands* blog tells us of the long journey from sickness to health. She gives us the medical reports, the ingredients of the chemo cocktails, and tells us what bilateral mastectomy really is like. It's an ordeal of course, but through it all she is supported by a loving family and good friends. Losing a breast doesn't make you any less of a woman, she tells us, since the boobs can be reconstructed.

I had nipple reconstruction last week. I hesitated in getting them. Let's face it, they aren't functional in any way imaginable. Did I need a surgical procedure yet again? I'm so glad I did it. I love them. They are so cute. It is the best thing

I have had done in this process. They make me feel a bit more complete and they magically turn chest lumps into breasts.

Twisty Faster is not impressed. This self-confessed 'patriarchy-blamer' from Texas had both her breasts removed and although she is 'doing extremely well', she is not in the mood for upbeat messages. Instead she tells us all about her 'chemically-induced anemia, menopause, baldness (including eyelashes and pubes!), assorted bodily function issues ... and the short daily burst of self-pity'. She is not having her breasts reconstructed. Instead she puts a picture of her scarred chest on the blog.

The only highlight of *Twisty Faster*'s ordeal comes when her lack of boobs gives her an opportunity to make a point about the pervasiveness of patriarchy. She's barred from her sister's country club pool, she tells us, unless she wears a swim top, but

it's loony for a chump like me to wear a top, since swimmy bras have all that fabric in the gazongal area, which fabric, if it is not filled up with gazonga, just poofs out there, conspicuously superfluous and unstreamlined. Whereas the case for bottoms can be made (for all sexes) in the interest of pube containage, a bra on a boob-free person amounts to an entirely gratuitous entanglement of the upper torso in pointless, gender-role-affirming cloth.

The new intimacy

In his novel, *Nineteen Eighty-Four*, George Orwell provided a nightmarish account of a future where all our movements and all our thoughts are closely monitored by the state. There is nowhere to hide and everything is observed by omnipresent eyes. Orwell's book was obviously based on the twentieth-century experiences of totalitarian regimes in Germany and the Soviet Union, yet today, it is clear that the twentieth-century experiences of liberal, capitalist regimes provide a more plausible future scenario. Here, people weren't forced to reveal themselves but chose to increasingly do so. It is not that Big Brother is listening but rather that all the small brothers can never shut up.

Blogs feed right into this trend. Blogs allow us to spill our hearts out all over our keyboards and then upload them straight onto the web. We blog naked. Blogs make it possible to live publicly and to live truthfully. It's like making a home for oneself in a shop window. We love, hate, masturbate and fornicate in full view of the passing public. Yuk!

Some people will never understand such self-revelatory urges. On the whole, they are people who are far too sure of themselves for their own good. They are people with positions to consider and reputations to protect. And white, middle-aged, middle-class, middle-brow males are vastly over-represented among them. Their identities branded onto their faces, they no longer remember what it was like to ask themselves who or what they are. To people like these the ever-presence of bloggers is a threat. 'You can't say that in your blog!' 'How can you say that in your blog?' 'You didn't say that in your blog, did you?'

In a showdown between truth-telling and bourgeois respectability, truth-telling must always win. The right to speak is more important than the need to keep up appearances. The desperation of a person searching for an identity has priority over the anxiety of a person worried about losing an identity. The presumption must always be in favour of the bloggers.

This is not to say that there are no limits to free speech. Even if we have a legal right to say a certain thing, and no fear of getting fired or reprimanded, there may still be good reasons to keep mum. One obvious consideration concerns the trade-off between online and offline experiences. Justin Hall blogged naked for 11 years but like many authors he eventually realized that he had to choose between his life and his art. He sacrificed his many virtual relationships for one deep, non-virtual, one. Having turned 30, he was ready to put his clothes back on.

As we constantly are reminded by traditional media, there are obvious risks associated with public nakedness. The problem of internet stalkers and pedophiles is real but considering the millions of self-revelatory items that exist on the web, the dangers are easily exaggerated. Teenagers need to posture, to write about themselves, and to socialize. Blogs and social networking sites are the perfect venues. Veterans of identity play, teenagers are actually more likely than their more literal-minded parents to understand the distinction between online and offline realities. OK, the parents don't like it. It makes them uncomfortable. But why pay so much attention to parental discomfort?

At the same time it's not surprising that people take offence at stuff written about them. Online statements have offline effects. If we piss people off we shouldn't be surprised that they are pissed off. It wasn't nice of Kyle to call Miranda names and he should apologize to her. Still, the people identified in this way need to learn to relax. Just as in the offline world, people will say all kinds of things about you, and there really isn't much you can do about it. The good news is that next to no one actually cares. Intimate revelations say more about what we have in common with everyone else than about what distinguishes us from others. Most lives aren't actually all that interesting.

The greatest threat against freedom of speech in a personal blog comes from people who are close to us. Censors, like rapists, tend to be people we know. They are members of our church, our bridge club or colleagues at work. Very often they are ex-husbands. If you decide, like our WoaCA bloggers, not to offend these people, that's certainly understandable but that doesn't necessarily mean that you have to stop writing. There are after all numerous ways of making yourself invisible. Take refuge behind a *nom de blog* and various literary devices. This way you can go on blogging as naked as you wish while we, the readers, get the continued pleasure of commenting on your figurative moles and your saggy, metaphorical bottom.

8

A Blogger's Manifesto

The European idea regarding freedom of speech was presented to us in the form of three inter-related promises. First, the promise regarding citizenship in a deliberative republic made up of equals. Second, the promise of personal growth and social progress through free thought and expression. Third, the radical promise that all privileges must be critically examined and that all people of authority must be able to justify their claims to power. Freedom of speech is the right to point out that the king is naked. And the president too.

In the eighteenth century the power of publicity was given a next-to metaphysical importance. Publicity was compared to a court which passed judgement on events, persons and social phenomena. But publicity was also a legislator that determined what kinds of actions are right and wrong. As Immanuel Kant put it, by imagining that our actions are publicly known and universally copied, we can determine what's morally acceptable. What if everyone did the same? What if everyone ate hamburgers on the subway and threw the wrapper on the floor?

Publicity, metaphysically understood, allows us to dispense with the services of external authorities. We can determine the law for ourselves even if gods are dead and kings have been dethroned. As Kant insisted, this kind of self-determination is the beginning of maturity for the human race.

This is a great argument. Sharp like a blade of steel on an aristocrat's neck. The only problem is that the ability to publicize things always was so terribly restricted. It only belonged to the privileged few, to the people who owned newspapers or to those who somehow managed to get past the editorial filters. The things that were exposed in the end were those the editors chose to expose.

Today, self-publication on the internet is dispensing with editors. As a result, for the first time ever, we can live in accordance with the principles we claim to believe in. Thanks to the blogging revolution the power of publicity is in every one's hands. Every minute of every day thousands of fingertips are reporting the actions of the high and the mighty straight onto the web. Everyone will soon be held accountable. Everything will soon be revealed. 'Watch it buddy, I'm blogging this!'

Immanuel Kant would have loved it. Voltaire too. Together, they would have blogged up a storm. It's up to us today to complete the project they started. We have found the last piece in the complicated jigsaw puzzle which is modern society. As we lovingly tend our blogs – posting, commenting and updating – world history is right by our side. The bloggers are riding the *Zeitgeist*.

Thought police *nouveau*

It took the old elites a long time to understand the challenge they were up against. These, after all, are people who only recently said goodbye to their typewriters. They don't surf the web much, except to very staid and official sites. They rely on 'engineers' and 'IT experts' to update the web pages of the companies they work for. They've read about *YouTube* and *Facebook* in the newspaper but they'd never dream of actually logging on and creating their own accounts.

Meanwhile, the foot soldiers of the blogging revolution gathered their pitchforks and pickaxes and prepared to march on the Bastille. They had no memory of typewriters, no respect for authority, and no sense of grammar. They treated the internet like it was their private playground. They talked irresponsibly about whatever came to their minds. Secrets were revealed, confidences were broken. The carefully controlled structures of information dissemination came crashing down. The bloggers went out of control.

When the gravity of the situation finally dawned on them, the old elites panicked. Some employees were fired for what amounted to nothing more than average water-cooler kvetching. Other employees were dooced for revealing 'insider information' which already was publicly known. Government advisers were sent forth, foaming at their mouths, to warn about 'conspiracies to keep people in a state of self-righteous rage'. Little old embroidery ladies were compared to 'Hitler's armies marching across Europe'. Universities, famous for their dedication to civil liberties, ordered their staff to 'take down and destroy' their blogs.

Then the old elites called in their henchmen: journalists, editors, internet companies, the people in Human Resources. The object was to warn the bloggers, in no uncertain terms, regarding the consequences that would befall them if they insisted on their rights. They came up with 'blog safely' manuals and 'voluntary codes' designed to curb the 'worst excesses' of the fad. Designed, that is, to make sure that the bloggers would forget about their new-found powers. 'This is your last chance', they warned. 'Stop offending us or we'll have to think up some draconian legislation.'

Surprisingly, internet companies often cooperated with the repression. They too censored and banned. The collusion of Google, Microsoft, Yahoo and Cisco Systems with the dictatorship in China is well known. What's more surprising is that Google cooperates also with French and German authorities in filtering websites, and that Microsoft censors blog accounts of

Chinese dissidents in the US too. On the whole, internet-service providers, web hosts and *YouTube*-type sites are scaredy cats. They'd rather close down a blog which someone complains about than lose one of their big accounts. Put a 'penisaurus' on your web page and you're carded. Private censorship is worse than state censorship in several respects. It's arbitrary, based on commercial considerations, and it rarely offers any effective form of redress.

If you happen to be a blogger working in a company or a university, it won't be long before you'll hear from the people in HR. They care about your well-being, they'll tell you, they care about you so much that they'll send motorcycle couriers to your door with invitations to go on disability leave. Investigations will be started and witnesses will be called. Rumours will be spread about your diminished faculties. They'll check your blog. They'll check it repeatedly, over and over, taking notes, comparing records and making backups on their hard disks. It's all very scary. Said Heather Armstrong, the original doocee:

> I am afraid that these people are watching everything I say here, ready to pounce on a single word, twist it, manipulate it, and then sue me again.

This is not freedom of speech. Freedom of speech requires the freedom from fear but there is today plenty of fear across workplaces and universities. As a result, people think twice before they start blogging. Self-censorship is probably more damaging in the end than explicit bans. It's the logic of customs officials everywhere – nab one offender and you'll scare ten potential ones.

The rationale for the repression is always the same. Bosses hate to have their authority undermined, they hate to be made fun of. They resent the fact that underlings now have independent means of communicating with each other and with the world. They worry about the corporate image, about the impact on stock prices, and at many universities they worry about student numbers. In Anglo-Saxon countries, after all, universities too are businesses.

If prospective students are told the truth about our university, the argument goes, they won't show up. Who is then going to pay for our research leaves?

The imperatives of the market reveal themselves to be our last taboo. Today, the bottom line is the only thing which is beyond criticism. In a democracy you can offend all you like as long as you don't say anything that has an impact on corporate profits. In this way, the market becomes a threat to freedom. The market is today the only authority that never needs to justify its power over us.

Faceless blogging

The easiest way to deal with most of these problems is to blog anonymously. If you only cut the connection between your online and your offline persona, they won't find you. Or at least, they won't find you as easily. Really, if you take some basic precautions, you'll be able to stay out of trouble. This, at least, is what all the 'blog safely' manuals are telling us.

There are certainly good reasons to follow this advice if you're blogging in a country like Iran, China or North Korea, or if you're employed by the Guantanamo Bay detention facility and you blog about what's going on at work. In places like these, there is important information that must be made public and it's crucial that they won't be able to shut you up. The identity of the messenger matters less than the content of the message.

In democracies too we might just decide that faceless blogging is safer. Anonymity means that you don't have to worry about being found out by family, friends and employers. After all, even if what we say is perfectly legal, there may be people out there who decide to come looking for us, dropping dog-do-do in our mailboxes and threaten our kids. Freedom of speech, we said, requires the freedom from fear and faceless blogging is great for reducing stress levels. If they can't connect your words to your face, they can't get you.

But anonymity is at the same time detrimental to democracy. For one thing anonymity makes it far easier to make irresponsible statements. You can be racist, sexist, ageist or overweightist and you will suffer no repercussions. You can deny the holocaust or the existence of Santa Claus or whatever. A debate between anonymous protagonists is for this reason likely to be far more vociferous.

Even more damaging, disembodied opinions are easy for traditional elites to dismiss. Anonymous sources just aren't very trustworthy. If no one knows who you are, they have no reason to listen to you. If you conceal your face, you speak with less authority. This is of course exactly the way elites want it to be. While they themselves never have to conceal their faces, they make fun of bloggers who are forced to speak anonymously. In this way, the semblance of freedom of speech is preserved while the arguments of the critics are undermined.

In general, disembodied opinions are unlikely to have much of an effect. By not being attachable to a particular person, they can't be socially located and for that reason they have no social significance. They are mere words, without the backing of a will and a force. They are political arguments with politics taken out of them.

It would be easy to come up with a piece of software that generated opinions at random and posted them on a blog. The programme would run through all the permutations allowable by a language and publish millions of different opinions online. You can even imagine political debates carried out with the help of such blogging machines. By leaving dissenting comments on other machine-generated blogs, a very vigorous political debate could be produced. It would all be very impressive. Vigorous debate is crucial for democracy, we have been taught, and this is a super-debate where all the words of the language are called upon to do battle with all others.

Yet this perfect democracy is of course a perfect dystopia. It is a society in which everything is said and nothing is meant; where messages have neither senders nor recipients and where political programmes are supported by no power. It's a perfect democracy, especially for elites who will find it easier than ever to lord it over the rest of us.

The new public sphere

Let's look closer at the public sphere which the internet has created. Clearly, what we call 'public' or 'common' is never settled once and for all. It is instead determined by the technology we use when communicating. It depends on who we can reach and how we can reach them. The public sphere of classical Athenian democracy was small since you had to rely on your own voice when communicating. But as a result of the rapid growth of book publishing and newspapers in the eighteenth century, public spheres were created that encompassed entire nations. It was in this public sphere that ideas regarding freedom of speech first were introduced.

The public sphere created by the printing press can perhaps be compared to a great auditorium in which all members of society are assembled. One by one various speakers enter the podium at the centre of the hall and address the important issues of the day. This is how a common agenda is set, how common problems are discussed and common solutions arrived at. This is the public space in which politics unfolds. We call it 'democracy' since each member of the audience has the right to vote on the issues discussed.

Looking back on it now, it's strange that so much was made of the 'freedom' which this public sphere was said to offer. What we are more likely to notice is the coercion involved. After all, there was only one podium and exceedingly few people were ever allowed to speak from it. People with money and organizational resources would elbow their way to the lectern and start haranguing us on their pet topics. As a result, we ask fewer common questions and look for fewer common answers. The rest of us were forced to listen to them whether we wanted to or not.

But now there is new technology and our notion of a public sphere is changing. The internet provides not one but an infinite number of podiums. If there are 70 million blogs in the world, there are 70 million public platforms to speak from. The internet also provides a far more equal playing field. Sure, there is a difference between my little blog and the website of the government or a multinational corporation, but the difference isn't all that great. Add a few funky plug-ins to your site and you'll be rocking with the best of them.

The problem is only that everyone suddenly seems to be speaking and no one seems to be listening. But you can't have a room in which 70 million people are talking at the same time. There is far too much confusion. As a result, people increasingly prefer to leave the great auditorium and join any of the thousands of far smaller rooms where quite specific conversations are going on. We all have websites that we check on a daily basis, our discussion forums and our blogs. Some of these are larger than the others but none encompasses anything like a majority of all citizens. As a result, we ask fewer common questions and look for fewer common answers. There is far less of a public sphere.

Here public speech doesn't have nearly the same authority it had in the old public sphere. Since there are so many voices, speech has become cheap. It's just a lot of people sounding off on one topic after another. The more web-savvy we get, the less importance we attach to individual statements. This is a problem for people who try to sell stuff online – spammers selling Viagra or Swiss watches. Or people trying to convince us of their political views.

The topics have also changed. The old editorial filters were designed to assure a great degree of universality. What was discussed in public was supposed to be relevant to everyone and understandable by everyone – at least to everyone over a certain age and level of education. This is no longer the case. Today no one can stop us from being private in public. We can use all the jargon we like, make inside jokes and drop hard-to-follow references. We are under no obligation to make sense.

Many of the topics are also intensely personal. People reveal themselves in public in order to be able to understand themselves better. They seek affirmation and recognition from an imagined readership. Compare the great Justin Hall and his whole hog blog. Some might refer to this as a 'Jerry Springerization' of the public sphere. On the internet, just like on daytime TV, it is only once private emotions are revealed in public that they are taken to be real. Asking for confirmation, and hoping to unburden themselves on others, people go on and on about the most intimate details of their lives.

In this way the distinction between a public and a private realm is blurred. That's probably OK since it was a very dubious dichotomy to begin with. Our identities were always publicly created and publicly maintained. Or rather, we were always made up of layers of identities, stacked on each other, with quite unclear relations between them. There was never a private realm of truth and a public realm of make-believe. On the contrary, the truth about us was often spoken in public and we very often lied to ourselves in the privacy of our own minds.

The new notion of a public sphere allows us to affirm this multiplicity. It provides plenty of room for a more fragile and ambiguous self. It recognizes the human need for identity-play. It admits that identities always are in the process of becoming, and that we never really know who we are.

There are of course those who are perfectly scathing about this transformation. They worry about the trivialization of politics and the lack of genuine communities. They lament the declining importance of politics and are nostalgic for the once almighty power of the state. How can democracy survive, they ask, if there is no sense of a common agenda? How can we call ourselves citizens if we no longer interact in the same public space? How do we even know who we are if there is no clear distinction between the public and the private?

People who worry about these things are invariably the ones who benefited from the old, and now quickly disappearing, order – the few privileged speakers and the guards who helped police the crowds in the great auditorium. The rest of us have far less to lose. For us the changes represent new opportunities. When the old order is weakened and its leaders are in disarray we just might have a chance of putting some better system in place.

Yet, it doesn't matter what we make of these changes. They will happen whether we approve of them or not. In fact, most of them have little to do with the internet or with blogs. The public sphere has been privatized and intimicized for decades, even centuries, already. The internet is an expression of this long-term trend but it is not its cause. The bloggers are riding the Zeitgeist, but they aren't directing it. So, let's stop whining and instead take another look at what freedom of speech possibly could mean under these conditions.

A new set of rules

The idea of freedom of speech, we said, originated in a public sphere which was organized around the printing press. Here, free speech was considered a right and it was combined with responsibilities. There were certain things you couldn't say, and if you did you'd get yourself into trouble. Except that the editors who policed the system usually made sure that things never got that far. They always erred on the side of caution, sacrificing your rights while saving your butt.

The rules that organize the public sphere in the digital era are quite different. There are no editors any more and no one can stop us from saying what we like. There are thousands of separate rooms rather than one large auditorium; words are ever-present and cheap; web-surfers are cynical and easily bored; people speak casually about whatever comes into their minds. Here, freedom of speech is not a right as much as an inevitability. There is no reason to accept any responsibilities, at least not if we settle for blogging anonymously and if we don't live in North Korea, China or Iran. We may *choose* to be responsible but no one can make us.

And this is the neat bit: the rules governing freedom of speech today aren't restrictions on what we can say. They aren't lists of warnings and admonitions. They aren't even lists of the demands that bloggers might make in return for some imaginary concessions. There is nothing to bargain over any more since there is nothing we want from people in authority that we can't get for ourselves. Instead the new set of rules specify the conditions which the old elites will have to accept if they are to survive in the new and vastly different environment. The digital revolution has already happened. Get used to it!

- Companies have to accept far more criticism from their customers. You can no longer get away with things you got away with in the past. Gripe sites and discussion forums will mercilessly expose your shenanigans. Of course some people will exaggerate and spread lies about you, but the only way you can counter that is to be even more forthcoming with information. You need to communicate with your customers far more honestly and more directly. Legal threats and intimidation won't work. In fact, they will spectacularly backfire. Customers with blogs, you will have to realize, are always right. Even when they're wrong they're right.

- Bosses and other corporate types – You must first learn to calm down. You must accept that underlings often complain about things even in well-run companies and that underlings with blogs are likely to do so online. Think of this as a great opportunity to finally hear what people are saying behind your back. Acquire the habit of listening also to negative comments and accept the challenges they present. These are excellent opportunities to improve your business. If you're English, stop worrying about corporate hierarchies and stop being so freakin' pompous. If you're American, stop worrying about the impact on share prices. Put together a generous policy on blogging that respects your employees and encourages them to express themselves online. A few enlightened companies are doing this already. And if you don't have a blogging policy, don't you dare fire anyone for what they write. To punish someone for breaking a non-existent law is tyranny. And don't you dare punish employees who engage in activities explicitly protected by the constitution. It's bad PR, it's nasty, and it won't stand up in court.

* University administrators – Get a copy of your university's statement on freedom of speech and spend a few moments actually reading it. Next, apply the principles to the way your university is run. If you come across a blog of a member of staff that 'publicly abuses his employer and his colleagues' consider yourself lucky to have people around who think for themselves and who aren't afraid of your authority. Consider hiring this person as a consultant on how to use the internet in order to communicate more effectively with prospective students. Count blogging towards promotions provided the blogs are frequently updated and sufficiently critical. Abandon the old corporate feel of your university's web pages and go for a far more personalized and interactive look. As a bare minimum, all academic staff must be required to be on *Facebook* and the university's President must be vlogging on *YouTube*. As for students, make sure they all have accounts on the university's own blogging server. Think up new ways in which blogs can be used in learning and assessments. Make social networking sites available in all dorms and in particular in locker rooms frequented by female soccer players. If you run a religious university, make sure the students use the web to learn about sin before you teach them about repentance. If you run a university which puts profits before principles, ask yourself why Judas Iscariot always gets such a bad rap.

- Bosses in both companies and universities – Stop spending your time scouring the web for compromising material. Stop reading our blogs over and over, and stop taking notes and comparing records. Can't you see you've created your own police department and department of censorship. Before you know it, you find yourself as the ruler of your own little North Korea.

- Politicians – Please read our blogs and discover what we really think of you. Please read our blogs and discover what we think of our society. Start blogging yourself and do it with feeling, like you actually cared. Lay off those fake internet-based publicity stunts and don't just post things when you're on the campaign trail. We want authentic messages clearly spoken. And don't forget that the government agencies you're in charge of are staffed with bloggers who observe what's going on and who are prepared to write about it. Protect whistle-blowing officials. Make it easy for them to blow their whistles online. If you're a hereditary monarch in a European country, have a manservant set up an account for you on the *Blogger* web page. It's not such a powerful technology but it's very user-friendly once it's up and running. Thank your subjects in your first post for paying your salary for all these years.

- People who are easily offended – My sincere apologies but this is a very bad time for you to be alive. Offence is all over the internet and there's more of it every day. If people like you are allowed to have your way, there just wouldn't be very much for the rest of us to talk about. We can't let you. We must stop you. If you're a Muslim suicide bomber, the Pope or a minister in the New Labour government, maybe you should consider going off to live somewhere else. Maybe you could seek asylum in a country where Google filters its search results. China comes to mind, or Iran, or maybe France.

- Women, handicapped people, people of minorities and other victims – Don't look at all the stupid online stuff. The rest of us don't and don't for a second think that the fact that something exists on the web means that it's officially endorsed or widely believed. It's just the same old prejudice we've been getting from taxi-drivers for years. By the way, thank you very much for your patience with the bullies. You are the ones paying the highest price for the freedom we all enjoy.

- Parents – If you haven't noticed already, your sons and your daughters are beyond your command. But please don't criticize what you can't understand. The carefully rendered walls of your suburban castle are leaking. One by one your family's best kept secrets are soaked up by the internet and piped around the world. Yes, it's very embarrassing. Yes, people in your church and your country club are reading. In fact, they can't get enough of the stuff. Then again you are reading what their children are saying online about them. Perhaps, it all evens out in the end. Perhaps, when everything's said and done we'll all realize just how much we all have in common. Maybe our new-found knowledge will be the beginning of a new kind of cross-suburban solidarity. Yes, there are indeed pedophiles online and other creepy people too. But before your repressive instincts get the better of you, sit down with your child and ask him or her to teach you what online communication is like. Perhaps you could even create an alternative online identity for yourself. Just for fun. Live a little.

- Girlfriends who get slagged off and other friends betrayed – If we google your name it is indeed possible to find a lot of compromising material about you. I never knew, for example, that you had a bad case of the claps back in 2003. Then again, according to WHO statistics, sexually transmitted diseases infect some 1 million people a day worldwide. You're not alone, you're not unique. In fact, you're not even all that interesting. Let the person who never had a brush with STDs cast the first stone. Take it philosophically. There are people out there who are chronicling your life for you. You are leaving a trace. For a more complete account of your life make sure that you add plenty of your own material.

Back online

Let's go back to our online pursuits. Reading a book now and then is great fun. After all, sometimes the internet is down and besides, you get tired of always staring at a screen. Still, there's no denying it, after spending some time offline you tend to get homesick for your web pages.

So what should we write about? It's not easy to come up with something juicy on a daily basis. Besides, our low readership is kind of depressing. But so what? If we simply start typing something will surely emerge. In the process of writing you'll learn to use your voice more confidently and you'll learn a great deal about yourself. There will come a day when you'll need that voice and that knowledge.

Try to give your constitutional rights a bit of a work-out. Test the system and find out where its limitations are. Our rights, like our voices, will weaken if they aren't used. Write about something that makes you really angry. Write about a person who really pisses you off. Next, write about someone you love and let us know why you love them. Finally, tell us who you are. How do you know you are that person and what other kind of a person could you possibly be? If nothing else, write about something funny that happened at work. Perhaps you'll get lucky, and some pompous colleague inadvertently will draw a penis on a whiteboard during a boring presentation.

And if you do get into trouble, rely on some basic guerrilla tactics. Duck, dive and dodge. Change items around or claim they never existed. Write in code, write in Bahasa Indonesia. Kick them once again on the shins, harder this time, and then run like hell. If they come looking for you, hide inconspicuously among ordinary internet users. Fight dirty; fight cowardly. Temporarily take down your blog, or rather, take it down temporarily for people reading it from certain computers. When you put it back up again, make sure it's mirrored in the ten countries in the world with the best record of defending civil liberties.

It's profoundly humiliating to be deprived of one's constitutional rights. And to your surprise some of your colleagues may take considerable pleasure in seeing you humiliated. But humiliation can be a source of great creative power. First, you get mad and then you get even. If nothing else, start blogging about it. Blog about it long, and blog about it good.

Think of your experience as an opportunity to teach your employer, your university, your family and friends, what freedom of speech means in an age of internet-based communication. And think of it as a way to test your commitment to modern society. If human rights depended on you, would you fight for them or would you rather not bother? And don't forget, in the end the bloggers are many and the censors are few. We will not be defeated. We'll never fall silent. The online revolution has only just begun.

Bibliography

The internet resources I have relied on in writing this book are listed in the book's blog at www.ringmar.net. In addition, I have consulted the sources below.

Chapter 1

There are many books on freedom of speech, not least by legal scholars. I found Cass Sunstein's *Democracy and the Problem of Free Speech* (Free Press, 1993) particularly enlightening. The historical overview draws on Jürgen Habermas' *The Structural Transformation of the Public Sphere* (Polity, 1992), Reinhart Koselleck's *Critique and Crisis* (MIT Press, 1998) and Alan S Kahan, *Aristocratic Liberalism* (Transaction Publishers, 2001). A good introduction to the distinction between publicity and secrecy is Sissela Bok, *Secrets: On the Ethics of Concealment and Revelation* (Vintage, 1989).

Chapter 2

The best survey of blogging use and creation in the US is Pew Internet & American Life Project, *Bloggers: A Portrait of the Internet's New Story-Tellers*. 19 July 2006. The stuff about 'narration and identity creation' draws heavily on my 'On the Ontological Status of the State', *European Journal of International Relations*, 2:4, 1996, pp. 439–66.

Chapter 3

The best introduction to the history of the LSE is Ralf Dahrendorf, *LSE: A History of the London School of Economics and Political Science 1895–1995* (Oxford University Press, 1995). On the dangers of expertise see James C Scott, *Seeing Like a State: How Certain Schemes to Improve Human Condition Have Failed* (Yale University Press, 1998) and Timothy Mitchell, *Rule of Experts: Egypt, Techno-Politics and Modernity*. (University of California Press, 2002). On what's wrong with political science see David M Ricci, *The Tragedy of Political Science: Politics, Scholarship and Democracy* (Yale University Press, 1987).

Chapter 4

My all-time favourite book on what a university is and should be is Friedrich Schleiermacher, *On the Academy* (Edwin Mellen, 1987). The contemporary tribulations of the academic profession are revealed in James Hynes, *Publish and Perish: Three Tales of Terror and Tenure* (Picador, 1998). An insider's account of the free speech movement in the US is provided by Donald A Downs in *Restoring Free Speech and Liberty on Campus* (Cambridge University Press, 2006). The reference to Hayek is to Friedrich A Hayek, *Fatal Conceit: The Errors of Socialism* (Routledge, 1991).

Chapter 5

The classical text on emotion management at work is Arlie Russell Hochschild, *The Managed Heart: Commercialization of Human Feeling* (University of California Press, 2003). On the classical workplace see Richard Sennett & Jonathan Cobb, *The Hidden Injuries of Class* (W. W. Norton, 1993). On the new workplace see Peter Cappelli, *The New Deal at Work: Managing the Market-Driven Workforce* (Harvard Business School Press, 1999) and Simon Head, *The New Ruthless Economy: Work and Power in the Digital Age* (Oxford University Press, 2005). On the distinction between markets and political action see Albert O Hirschman, *Exit, Voice and Loyalty: Responses to Decline in Firms, Organizations and States* (Harvard University Press, 2006).

Chapter 6

For the introduction on oligopoly and news distortion by US media, I've learned from James Fallows, *Breaking the News: How the Media Undermine American Democracy* (Vintage, 1997) and Douglas Kellner, *Media Spectacle and the Crisis Of Democracy: Terrorism, War, and Election Battles* (Paradigm, 2005). The blogging soldiers in Iraq are discussed in Matthew Currier Burden, *Blog of War: Front-Line Dispatches from Soldiers in Iraq and Afghanistan* (Simon & Schuster, 2006). A good introduction on hate speech is Jon B Gould, *Speak No Evil: The Triumph of Hate Speech Regulation* (University of Chicago Press, 2005). Francisco Panizza provides an overview of populism in *Populism and the Mirror of Modernity* (W. W. Norton, 2005).

Chapter 7

Sissela Bok covers much of the same territory in her *Secrets: On the Ethics of Concealment and Revelation* (Vintage, 1989) – but of course from the point of view of a pre-internet perspective. Paul Ricœur discusses the role of confessions in *Freud and Philosophy: An Essay on Interpretation* (Yale University Press, 1977). On meaning and story-telling in the face of death see Zygmunt Bauman, *Mortality, Immortality and Other Life Strategies* (Stanford University Press, 1993). An outstanding collection of articles on the private/public distinction is *Public and Private in Thought and Practice: Perspectives on a Grand Dichotomy*, edited by Jeff Weintraub & Krishan Kumar (University of Chicago Press, 1997).

Chapter 8

The discussion of technology draws on Elizabeth L Eisenstein, *The Printing Revolution in Early Modern Europe* (Cambridge University Press, 2005); Jack Goody, *The Logic of Writing and the Organization of Society* (Cambridge University Press, 1987) and Benedict Anderson, *Imagined Communities: Reflections on the Origin and Spread of Nationalism* (Verso, 2006). The idea of a public sphere is famously developed in Jürgen Habermas' *The Structural Transformation of the Public Sphere* (Polity, 1992). I've previously discussed the 'privatization' of the public sphere in 'The Idiocy of Intimacy', *British Journal of Sociology*, 49:4, 1998, pp. 534–49 and that article in turn drew heavily on Richard Sennett, *The Fall of Public Man* (Penguin, 2003). Again see the Weintraub and Kumar volume regarding the private/public distinction.